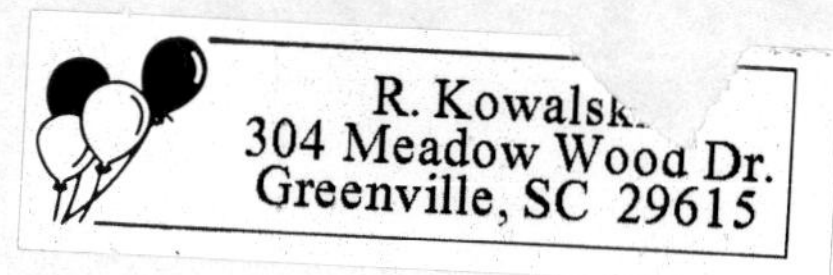

Opening the New Testament

OPENING THE NEW TESTAMENT

by

H. Robert Cowles

Christian Publications
Camp Hill, Pennsylvania

Christian Publications
3825 Hartzdale Drive, Camp Hill, PA 17011

The mark of ✝ vibrant faith

Library of Congress Catalog Card Number: 84-72468

ISBN: 0-87509-357-4
Unless otherwise indicated, all Bible quotations are taken from the *New International Version*, copyright © 1978 by the New York International Bible Society and used by permission of Zondervan Bible Publishers.

Printed in the United States of America

Contents

Introduction

(To be read before you begin your study of chapter 1)

IF YOU ARE ALREADY acquainted with the companion volume, *Opening the Old Testament*, you will have a good idea of my method of operation.

This introduction will present a brief overview of the New Testament and its background and offer a few suggestions for getting the most out of your textbook and the course in New Testament survey.

Each of the 13 chapters will then take up a particular section of the New Testament, looking in sharper focus at the contents of the book or books within that section.

If, as sometimes happens, the class you are in must limit itself to 12 rather than 13 lessons, your teacher may wish to combine chapters 4 and 6 (covering Romans and Galatians—two books of a somewhat similar theme). Or your teacher may telescope chapters 11 and 12, considering all 8 general letters (some of them rather short) in a single lesson.

Some background information

In case you have not studied the Old Testament, it will be helpful to look for a moment at what precedes the New. Someone once put together the following interesting comparison:

When we refer to the Old Testament, we refer to 39 books written by close to 30 authors over a span of a thousand years. Whether reciting history (generally, Genesis through Esther), speaking prophetically to the then-generation and to all the generations to come (Isaiah through Malachi), or reflecting the kaleidoscopic moods of Israel through poetry (most of the rest), the Old Testament displays a remarkable unity. This unity is a strong evidence that the authors wrote under the inspiration of God Himself.

After the early chapters of Genesis, the first Old Testament book, most of the rest of the Old Testament is an account of God's dealing with Israel, a nation He chose for a unique relationship with Himself. That record begins with the call of Abraham to leave what is now Iran and to journey west to Canaan (present-day Israel), a land God promised to give to Abraham's descendents.

The fulfillment of that promise took shape slowly. Abraham had a son, Isaac, who had a son, Jacob, who had 12 sons. Famine conditions in Canaan forced the family, then a clan of 70 people, into Egypt. Rather than return to Canaan after conditions there improved, they remained in Egypt for four centuries, multiplying to a vigorous young nation of 2 to 3 million people.

The king of Egypt began to look on Israel as a threat and subjected the people to slavery. God specially commissioned Moses to lead them from Egypt's clutches in one of the largest national migrations in world history. When they eventually reached Canaan, they overpowered the people living there and began the task of nation-building.

Saul, Israel's first king, was a disappointment. David, who followed him, did much to establish Israel as a major Middle East power, and his son Solomon further built the nation and also constructed its first permanent temple to Jehovah God.

But material prosperity and national achievement brought in their wake spiritual retrogression. In punishment God divided the kingdom into north and south, Israel and Judah. And when even that failed to check the waywardness of the people, He permitted them to be carried into captivity by the Assyrians and the Chaldeans (Babylonians).

Many of them returned to Canaan ultimately, weaned from their idolatry. But the days of national grandeur were gone and unrecoverable. Israel was at best a remnant of her former glory and the victim of a fast-changing political climate as Greece and later Rome rose to power.

In the fullness of time

At least in the traditional sequence of its books, the New Testament begins with the announcement and birth of Jesus Christ and ends not quite a century later with His church beginning to be firmly established in the Roman world.

One of the New Testament writers—the apostle Paul—declares that Jesus Christ came "when the time had fully come" (Galatians 4:4). What were the converging circumstances which made that particular point in history so propitious?

Rome was the dominant empire by this time, with Caesar Augustus at the helm. Rome's conquest of Greece was not so distant, but there were many residual influences from the remarkable era of Greek domination.

Greece was more than an empire, more than a culture. It was a spirit. It was the spirit of Plato and Aristotle, the spirit of physical prowess and intellectual pursuit. Of Athens in the fifth century before Christ it has been said, "One city gave birth to more great men of the first rank than the whole world has ever produced in any equal period."

But that profusion of philosophy and science had left in its wake a spiritual vacuum and pervasive despair. As one writer of that period expressed it, "We are so much at the mercy of chance that Chance is our god." People steeped in the spirit of Greece were ready for the liberating Good News of a Savior and Lord, Jesus Christ.

The Greek language, in the first century still the lingua franca of the Roman world, meant that the Good News could be communicated readily throughout the area. And the Old Testament Scriptures, written originally in Hebrew, had been translated into Greek.

Rome, too, had made its contribution to the spread of the gospel. Her military superiority had ushered in an unprecedented era of peace, called the Pax Romana. Her laws assured protection to Roman citizens. Her roads, well patrolled, offered mobility to those who would be taking the gospel into the far reaches of the empire. Her cities—large commercial complexes such as Antioch, Ephesus, Corinth, Philippi—became "key cities" for the Christian mission. Moreover, there were enclaves of Jews in every major city of the empire—a boon to evangelists such as Paul who needed an entree like that as they approached a new city with their priceless Good News.

The New Testament books

The New Testament consists of 27 books, some of them of

considerable length, others less than a page long. We are indebted to eight writers—four known to us from the text (Paul, James, Peter, Jude) and four known from tradition (Matthew, Mark, Luke, John)—(the letter to the Hebrews is of undetermined authorship, despite the inscription in many King James Version Bibles attributing it to Paul the apostle).

The 27 books, together with author or probable author and approximate date of writing are here listed under five categories:

Four Gospels	Writer	Date of Writing
Matthew	Matthew	A.D. 45–55
Mark	Mark	50–68
Luke	Luke	60
John	John	85–95
One history book		
Acts	Luke	62
Thirteen letters by Paul		
Romans	Paul	55–56
1 Corinthians	Paul	55
2 Corinthians	Paul	56
Galatians	Paul	48–58
Ephesians	Paul	60–61
Colossians	Paul	60–61
1 Thessalonians	Paul	50–51
2 Thessalonians	Paul	51
1 Timothy	Paul	63
2 Timothy	Paul	67
Titus	Paul	65
Philemon	Paul	60–61
Eight general letters		
Hebrews	Not known	65–70
James	Jesus' brother	45
1 Peter	Peter	63–65

2 Peter	Peter	65–67
1 John	John	85–90
2 John	John	85–90
3 John	John	85–90
Jude	Jude	67–85
One book of prophecy		
Revelation	John	90-95

As you will notice, Bible scholars are inclined to believe that James may have been the earliest New Testament book, followed closely by First and Second Thessalonians, considered the earliest of Paul's letters. Mark's was probably the earliest Gospel, although the three so-called synoptic Gospels (meaning from the same general viewpoint, and referring specifically to Matthew, Mark and Luke) were likely all written in the space of not more than 20 years. John's Gospel, which differs markedly in aim and viewpoint from the other three, was likely written quite late in the first century, as were also his three letters and Revelation.

Assuming that these dates are reasonably accurate, the New Testament was started some 16 years after the crucifixion* and was concluded before the century ended.

Compared with the nearly 4,000 years the Old Testament covers, the New is extremely restricted, spanning less than a full century. The Old Testament, as we have noted, was about 1,000 years in preparation (from the time of Moses, who wrote the first five books, until Malachi, who wrote the last). By contrast, the New Testament was written in about 50 years.

---

*Because of a miscalculation in the Gregorian calendar, the year A.D. 1 and Jesus' birth did not really coincide. More than likely Jesus was born in 4 B.C., and thus His crucifixion 33 years later would have been in A.D. 29, or possibly A.D. 30.

To whom was the New Testament written?

Those are the technical details. Of greater practical interest to us is the intended readership. To whom was the New Testament addressed?

It seems clear that the synoptic Gospels (Matthew, Mark, Luke) were written so that the young church might know what someone has called the "saving facts" and the teachings of the Living Jesus. They are more than history, more than diary, more than biography. They are Gospels—the Good News of Jesus Christ. As we will see, each of the three was written from a specific viewpoint, but basically for Christians.

John wrote his Gospel "that you may believe that Jesus is the Christ, the Son of God, and that by believing you may have life in his name" (20:31). He selects just seven faith-building miracles performed by Jesus during His ministry on earth, concluding his account with Passion Week and some of the Master's final instruction to His disciples, and the resurrection.

It is in John's Gospel that we find what has been called the Golden Text of the Bible: "For God so loved the world that he gave his one and only son, that whoever believes in him shall not perish but have eternal life" (3:16). John equates believing on Jesus with receiving Him: "To all who received him, to those who believed in his name, he gave the right to become the children of God—children born not of natural descent, nor of human decision or a husband's will, but born of God" (1:12-13).

Therefore to be born again (another of John's terms) as a child of God, it is necessary to believe on Jesus Christ—that is, to receive Him. This act presupposes a genuine sorrow for the sins you have committed and a resolution to turn from the ways of sin to the way of Christ.

The book of Acts contains the history of the early church.

Like the first three Gospels, it too is written to Christians.

The letters of Paul are addressed either to specific churches (at Rome, at Corinth, in Galatia, etc.) or to specific individuals (Timothy, Titus, Philemon). The general epistles are written to believers in various geographical areas. The Revelation is addressed primarily to seven churches in Asia Minor named in chapters 2 and 3, but the prophetic message that follows seems much more universal in its intended readership and belongs to the church of all ages.

To get the most from this course

If you have been able to read this Introduction and chapter 1 before your class meets for the first time, you will be "in sync" with your teacher and ready to absorb the additional information he or she has for you each week and to enter into the class discussion.

At the beginning of each lesson are seven Bible readings, one for each day of the week. Read those *prior* to the class session. For example, the readings at the beginning of chapter 1 should be read the week *before* chapter 1 is studied in class. These readings will help you to get a feel for some of the content of the particular book or books under consideration that week.

At the end of each lesson are two to five "Second mile" questions or topics. They are designed to help you personally delve a little deeper into the subject under consideration.

Although the Bible is an inexhaustible treasure of information, the person who approaches it merely from the intellectual vantage point is depriving himself or herself of the Bible's main value. It is God's written communication with mankind, and through it God wants to bring us into a spiritual relationship with Himself. Just as the Old Testament predicted the coming of a Savior, so the Gospels (the word means Good News) report His advent, His ministry on earth, His death by crucifixion, His resurrection.

But knowing in an intellectual way these facts is not sufficient. God wants to make us His sons and daughters through faith in Jesus Christ.

The Good News is that Christ died for our sins and was buried and rose again, and that by faith in Him we become sons and daughters of God—spiritual children in whose lives God resides by means of the Spirit of Christ Jesus.

Pleasant studying!

1

The Record of Jesus Christ
Matthew, Mark, Luke

Into the Word Each Day

1.	Matthew 1:18-25	Jesus is born
2.	Matthew 5:1-12	The Beatitudes
3.	Mark 8:34-38	Being a disciple
4.	Mark 10:13-16	Jesus and the children
5.	Luke 23:32-46	Jesus is crucified
6.	Luke 24:1-8	The resurrection
7.	Matthew 28:16-20	The Great Commission

MATTHEW, MARK AND LUKE'S GOSPELS are called synoptic because they present the same general, rather comprehensive view of the life and ministry of Jesus Christ. John's Gospel, as we will see in the next chapter, is by contrast quite different in viewpoint and purpose.

Matthew was one of Jesus' 12 disciples—a tax collector before Jesus called him (Matthew 9:9). He would therefore be expected to have a first-hand recollection of the events taking place during Jesus' three years of ministry in Galilee and Judea. Undoubtedly in private conversations Jesus had shared with His disciples details of His birth and early life.

Mark and Luke were not original disciples. Scholars generally take the view that Mark, who may have been only a teenager during the years of Jesus' ministry on earth, received his information from Peter, with whom he was associated in ministry. Church "fathers," such as Papias, assert that Mark was both Peter's disciple and interpreter. Peter refers to him as "my son Mark" (1 Peter 5:13), implying not biological but spiritual kinship—possibly one of Peter's converts. His dependence on Peter for information is evident in many places in his Gospel, such as the detailed account of Peter's denial of Christ in the courtyard of the high priest (Mark 14:66–72). Probably Mark is the "young man" (Mark 14:51) who fled when Jesus' captors tried to apprehend him.

Not only did Mark in all probability produce the earliest Gospel, but he was likely the youngest of the New Testament writers.

Doctor Luke

Luke, a medical practitioner, was a later associate of Paul. Paul refers to him as "our dear friend Luke, the doctor" (Colossians 4:14). This educated patrician, probably a Gentile, was associated with Paul's evangelistic team beginning in Troas and thereafter intermittently, including his shipwreck and ultimate arrival in Rome. Although not an eyewitness of Jesus' life and ministry, in true scientific fashion he "carefully investigated" the available data. He begins his Gospel by saying:

"Many have undertaken to draw up an account of the things that have been fulfilled among us, just as they were handed down to us by those who from the first were eyewitnesses and servants of the word. Therefore, since I myself have carefully investigated everything from the beginning, it seemed good also to me to write an orderly account" (1:1–3).

Luke's two-volume work (volume 2 is the book of Acts) is of a high literary quality—the best of any in the New Testament.

Matthew wrote especially to Jewish Christians. He quotes frequently from the Old Testament. He includes details, as for example Jesus' descent from David and Abraham (1:1), that are important to Jews. Matthew emphasizes the kingship of Jesus: His royal birth at Bethlehem; His forerunner, John the Baptist; His ministry and ultimate rejection by His own people; His predictions of His second coming in power and great glory.

If Matthew writes to Jews, Mark writes to Gentile believers. He takes pains to explain Jewish customs that would be totally familiar to Jewish readers. Mark puts stress upon the servanthood of Jesus. His Gospel is a record of the *doings* of Jesus more than His sayings. Mark's narrative is fast-paced and filled with action.

Luke writes especially to educated Christians, both Jew and Gentile. He presents Jesus as the Son of Man, the perfect human being. He goes into great detail concerning His birth to the virgin Mary. The expression "Son of Man" occurs frequently in Luke's Gospel, the key verse being "The Son of Man came to seek and to save what was lost" (19:10).

Matthew

The gospel of Matthew, as we said, is directed especially to Jewish readers. As such it forms a bridge from the Old Testament to the New. Note in Matthew 1:22–23, for example, how Matthew makes sure his readers see in Jesus the fulfillment of the Old Testament prophecy: "All this took place to fulfill what the Lord had said through the prophet: 'The virgin will be with child and will give birth to a son, and they will call him Immanuel'—which means, 'God with us'"—a reference to Isaiah 7:14.

Matthew takes great pains to relate the life of Jesus to the Scriptures of his day—the Old Testament. He quotes the Old

Testament 41 times, 37 times noting the fulfillment of a prediction made centuries earlier. Matthew thereby assures his readers that the ministry of Jesus, thoroughly biblical, demonstrated God's faithfulness to His people and His Word.

Although Israel had been in subjection for most of the previous five centuries, the hope that her fortunes would turn continued to be the fond dream of every Jew. Notice, for instance, the question of Jesus' own disciples after His resurrection: "'Lord, are you at this time going to restore the kingdom to Israel?'" (Acts 1:6). The disciples regarded Jesus as the one who would immediately turn Israel around. They did not yet understand that first Jesus' kingdom was spiritual—and open to Gentile as well as Jew. Only at the consummation of the age would it be also political as Jesus reigns in righteousness over the whole earth (see Revelation 20:1–6).

It is Matthew who has the Magi asking, "'Where is the one who has been born king of the Jews?'" (2:2). It is Matthew who traces Jesus' genealogy back to King David (1:1). It is especially Matthew who records Jesus' parables about His kingdom.

Systematic progression

It is always helpful if we can see in a book some kind of systematic progression. We have such in Matthew. The main body of the book is really divided into five discourses arranged primarily by topic rather than by event.

1. The Sermon on the Mount (5:1—7:29)
2. The commissioning of the 12 disciples (10:1–42)
3. The parables of the kingdom (13:1–53)
4. The meaning of greatness and forgiveness (18:1–35)
5. The "Olivet discourse" concerning the future (24, 25)

These discourses, plus an introduction covering Jesus' birth and baptism, and the concluding chapters covering His passion and resurrection, constitute the book.

In chapter 21 we have the description of Jesus' triumphal entry into Jerusalem at the beginning of Passion Week. Matthew points out that all of this was in fulfillment of an Old Testament prophecy (Zechariah 9:9) concerning Israel's future King:

> *"Say to the Daughter of Zion,*
>   *'See, your king comes to you,*
> *gentle and riding on a donkey,*
>   *on a colt, the foal of a donkey'"*
>
> *Matthew 21:5.*

In the Lord's Prayer (Matthew 6:9–13), Jesus taught His disciples to say, "'"your kingdom come."'" The expression "kingdom of heaven" occurs 33 times, "kingdom of God" 40 times, and the word "kingdom" over 50 times. The kingdom of heaven is the theme of 10 of the 14 parables recorded by Matthew. And in the Olivet discourse concerning the end of the age, Matthew notes that Jesus told His disciples, "'This gospel of the kingdom will be preached in the whole world as a testimony to all nations, and then the end will come'" (24:14).

Clearly and unmistakably, Matthew etches an inspired picture of Jesus, not only King of the Jews (2:2) but Lord of the universe (28:18).

Mark

Mark's is the Gospel of action. Note his use of words like "at once," "as soon as," "immediately." Mark spends little time telling us what Jesus said. But in a way none of the other writers do, Mark lets us see Jesus in motion—looking in anger on the synagogue audience who would rather see one of their number continue with a "shriveled hand" than to violate the law against working on the Sabbath (3:1–6); standing up in the stern of the storm-tossed boat and commanding the Sea of Galilee, "'Quiet! Be still!'" (4:39).

Five of the 16 chapters deal with the week of Jesus' Passion, a higher proportion than Matthew and Luke devote to the same events.

In keeping with the sense of action, we can divide Mark into Jesus' seven preaching tours:

1. First tour of Galilee (1:14—4:34)
2. Tour of Decapolis (Ten Cities) (4:35—5:43)
3. Second tour of Galilee (6:1–29)
   Retreat to the desert (6:30–52)
4. Third tour of Galilee (6:53—7:23)
5. Tour of the North Country (7:24—9:29)
6. Fourth tour of Galilee (9:30–50)
7. Tour of Perea and Judea (10:1–52)

In Jerusalem (11:1—16:20) (Although 16:19–20 is ancient, there is considerable doubt that it was a part of Mark's original Gospel.)

A comparison of the three synoptic Gospels indicates differences in the placing of some events. These differences show that the evangelists did not attempt a strict chronology in the life of Jesus. Nevertheless, scholars are inclined to believe that Mark adheres most closely to a chronological sequence.

Luke

Luke, as we said, was directed particularly to the educated classes. The Greeks attached great importance to human and physical perfection. Luke portrays Jesus as the perfect Man. He goes into greater detail than Matthew concerning Jesus' birth. He alone records an incident from Jesus' boyhood. He informs us that "Jesus grew in wisdom and stature and in favor with God and men" (2:52).

More than the other Gospel writers, Luke concentrates on the prayers of Jesus. For example, all the writers mention Jesus' baptism, but only Luke tells us that Jesus was praying at the time of his baptism (5:21).

Luke reveals Jesus as the Son of Man. He emphasizes the universality of the gospel—especially to the "outsiders" such as the poor, the women, the non-Jew. Here is one outline of Luke's Gospel:

1. The preparation of the Son of Man (1:5—4:13)
2. His Galilean ministry (4:14—9:50)
3. His Perean ministry (9:51—18:30)
4. His Jerusalem ministry (18:31—21:38)
5. His death and resurrection (22:1—24:53)

What the synoptics have in common

We have pointed out some of the differences in the accounts of the three synoptic writers. Although *anything* recorded for us in the Word of God has its importance, it is instructive to see what all three writers emphasized in common.

All three record the announcement of Messiah Jesus by John the Baptist, Jesus' forerunner.

All three cover

Jesus' baptism

His temptation in the wilderness

His transfiguration

His trial, death, burial

His resurrection and empty tomb

His Great Commission (if the authenticity of Luke 16:19–20 is accepted)

In each, Jesus' teaching and miracles occupy a major portion of the text. In these three Gospels at least 30 different parables are preserved for us.

If these three writers—Matthew, Mark and Luke—seek to acquaint us with the life of Jesus Christ, what sort of a composite picture do we get?

We see a miracle Child whose Father was God, born in extremely untoward circumstances, obedient to His parents. Leaving the quiet of Nazareth in Galilee at age 30, he launched a public ministry of preaching and healing and discipling a group of 12 rather unlikely men, 11 of whom would be His apostles to carry on His ministry after He had left the earth again.

We see a Man whose miracles of healing the sick, of feeding the hungry attracted a large following, especially in Galilee, but a Man who at the same time incurred the displeasure of the religious leaders in Jerusalem, who ultimately incited the people to call for His crucifixion.

We see a Man who claimed His purpose on earth was to seek and to save the lost; who in His death on the cross was not the victim of Jewish jealousy and Roman savagery so much as He was the Savior who voluntarily laid down His life to atone for the sins of mankind.

We see a Man who in His resurrection from the dead proved beyond a doubt His deity, leaving His followers with a commission to go into all the world and make disciples of all nations.

This is the Jesus whom Matthew, Mark and Luke portray. With the Roman centurion present at Jesus' crucifixion we must confess in all honesty: "'Surely he was the Son of God!'" (Matthew 27:54)—except that we say it in the present tense, for Jesus ever lives.

In our next chapter we shall look at what another of Jesus' disciples thought about Him. John begins where the other three evangelists conclude and presents Jesus not simply as the King of Israel, the suffering Servant, or the Son of Man, but as the true Son of God.

"Second mile" questions and topics

1. Skim Luke's Gospel. List the references Luke makes to Jesus at prayer. Why do you suppose Jesus felt the need to pray?

2. In Mark 4:1—5:20 we have the events in one busy 24 hours of Jesus' life. Imagine yourself a spectator in the events of that day and night and morning. What do you think would be your opinion of who Jesus was?

3. All three synoptists (Matthew, Mark, Luke) are careful to report Jesus' resurrection from the dead and the empty tomb. Read Matthew 28:1–15; Mark 16:1–8 and Luke 24:1–48. Do the reports seem fabricated? Or do they seem honest, factual? Note: Jesus' resurrection is at the very heart of the gospel. As Paul later says, "If Christ has not been raised [from the dead], our preaching is useless and so is your faith" (1 Corinthians 15:14).

2

Jesus, Son of God
John

Into the Word Each Day

THE THREE SYNOPTISTS—Matthew, Mark and Luke—have looked at the life of Jesus Christ, or at least His ministry years, as a whole. They present an orderly overview of Jesus' public years.

John is even more selective in his account of Jesus' life. He contents himself with just seven miracles of the hundreds and even thousands that Jesus must have worked in His ministry on earth. John wants to fill us not simply with facts but with faith. More than a hundred times he uses the word "believe."

If Matthew looks at Jesus as King, Mark as Servant and Luke as Son of Man, John sees Him as Son of God. Jesus' deity is the focus of John. He has written his Gospel so that we "may believe that Jesus is the Christ, the Son of God, and that by believing [we] may have life in his name" (John 20:31).

Jesus embodies Old Testament models

John observes that Jesus was the fulfillment of a number of Old Testament models or types.

1. The Tabernacle, where God dwelt among His people: "The Word became flesh and lived [literally, tabernacled] for a while among us" (John 1:14).

2. The Passover lamb. John the Baptist cries out as he sees Jesus approaching, "'Look, the Lamb of God, who takes away the sin of the world!'" (John 1:29).

3. Jacob's ladder or stairway at Bethel (see Genesis 28:10–12). Jesus told Nathanael, "'You shall see heaven open, and the angels of God ascending and descending on the Son of Man'" (John 1:51).

4. The bronze snake, or "brass serpent," as the King James Version terms it (see Numbers 21:9). Israel had sinned, and to punish them God sent "venomous snakes." Many of the people died. Repentant, they begged for relief. And at God's direction Moses made a bronze snake and mounted it on a pole. When the snake-bitten people looked at the serpent on the pole, they lived.

The episode becomes a nearly perfect illustration of Jesus' ministry on earth. "'As Moses lifted up the snake in the desert, so the Son of Man must be lifted up, that everyone who believes in him may have eternal life'" (John 3:14). Looking requires no particular intellectual effort. And note the similarity between a bronze snake on a pole and the crucified Savior on a cross.

5. The heavenly manna that sustained Israel during her journey from Egypt to Canaan (see Exodus 6:13–16). The true bread from heaven, Jesus says, "'is he who comes down from heaven and gives life to the world'" (John 6:33).

6. Water from the rock (Exodus 17:1–6), which refreshed Israel. Jesus declared, "'If a man is thirsty, let him come to

me and drink. Whoever believes in me, as the Scripture has said, streams of living water will flow from within him'" (John 7:37–38).

John gives us more

Although John's purpose is to select certain miracles that prove Jesus' deity, in doing so he has preserved facets of Jesus' ministry that Matthew, Mark and Luke omit.

For example, John refers to four passovers (2:13; 5:1; 6:4 and 11:55 ff.). Clearly this means that Jesus' public ministry stretched at least through three full years, rather than the little more than one year covered by the other three writers.

There is another striking difference in the scope of John's Gospel. Mark begins with Jesus' public ministry, Matthew and Luke take us back to Jesus' birth, but John goes to the beginning of time, and beyond, to let us know that Jesus was "with God and . . . was God"—the eternal Word or Expression of God.

Bishop B.F. Westcott has calculated that 92 percent of the material in the Gospel of John does not occur in the other three Gospels.

The writer and when he wrote

There was never much question in the early church that the Gospel was really the work of John, Jesus' "beloved disciple" and the apostle who outlived all the others. It is marked by detailed episodes witnessed only by Jesus' 12 disciples, such as the conversation between Jesus and His disciples after the woman of Samaria had returned into the city to get her "husband" (see John 4:27–38).

That John wrote his Gospel rather late in the first century is not only the consistent testimony of early Christian writers, but is borne out by internal evidence that presupposes some knowledge of the other Gospels. For example, John says little about Jesus' Galilean ministry, on which the other three writers concentrate. A date between A.D. 85 and A.D. 95 is a fair guess.

By this date, heresies were creeping into the church. Gnostic teachers (we will look at Gnosticism more closely in chapter 7) were sowing seeds of doubt concerning the deity of Jesus Christ. Such a Gospel as John's would be an appropriate answer to those who were challenging Jesus' claim to be the Son of God.

The church was by then approximately 50 years old. It had evolved from a predominantly Jewish entity to a predominantly Gentile entity—thanks in large part to the first church council in Jerusalem and the overruling of the Judaizers (more about that in the next chapter when we discuss Acts 15). Its leadership was second generation, a transition that frequently marks a cooling from the white-heat fervor of the founding generation. Only John remained as a link with the beginnings.

The seven signs

To assure his readers that Jesus is truly the Son of God, John selects seven miraculous "signs" from the Savior's life.

1. *The water changed to wine (2:1–11).* According to John, this was the first miracle in Jesus' public ministry. It is interesting, if not significant, that it took place at a social function—a wedding at Cana, north of Nazareth, to which Jesus had been invited as well as Jesus' mother (the absence of any mention of Joseph here or in other references to Mary causes Bible scholars to believe that he had died by that time).

Note Mary's dependence on Jesus (2:3). His reply, almost disrespectful in the King James translation, was not really so, as the newer translations indicate.

Jesus' miracle demonstrated His power over the mundane. Running out of wine was no world-stopping tragedy, but it was extremely embarrassing for the wedding sponsors. Yet even in such a circumstance, Jesus demonstrated His willingness—and His ability—to help.

2. *The healing of the nobleman's son (4:46–54).* This second sign was an emergency much more significant. The life of a boy hung in the balance. Anyone who has had children can enter into the concern of this anxious father. But more than that, this man is called a "royal official," and therefore he was a man of influence and power.

The official had a dual problem. Not only was his boy sick, but he was sick in Capernaum (4:46), and Jesus was again visiting Cana—a good 16 miles as the crow flies. The man seems to have had no doubt that Jesus could heal his son. It was only a question of His willingness to make such a lengthy trip on foot.

Jesus said, " 'Your son will live' " (4:50). Could it be that this One who had power to heal miraculously had power over distance as well? It was a new step of faith for the official. But Jesus had spoken and he believed. On his way home he was met by servants who informed him that the crisis was over. Inquiring of them as to exactly when the change came, he discovered that it was at precisely the time Jesus had assured him his son would live.

3. *The healing of the disabled man (5:2–9).* The next sign selected by the evangelist related to a rather pitiful scene. "A great number of disabled people" had gathered at Bethesda Pool near Jerusalem's Sheep Gate. They were physical castoffs, anxious for healing in the waters of the pool.

A 38-year-old invalid caught the Master's attention. " 'Do you want to get well?' " Jesus asked him (5:6). The man, thinking only of the pool and its reputed healing power, probably expected Jesus to help him to be first in when the waters stirred. But Jesus had a better plan.

"'Get up! Pick up your mat and walk,'" Jesus commanded (5:8). At once the man was cured and did as Jesus ordered. Here was a demonstration of Jesus' power over time. There was no need to wait for the waters to be stirred. Jesus could work at any moment.

4. *The feeding of the 5,000 (6:1–14)*. This miracle is recorded in all four Gospels. It was the most "public" of Jesus' signs, for an estimated 7,000–10,000 people were amply fed (Matthew informs us there were women and children in addition to the 5,000 men).

The miracle represented Jesus' power over quantity. The boy with the "'five small barley loaves and two small fish'" had *something*; divine multiplication made it feed a multitude.

5. *Jesus' walking on water (6:15–21)*. If the feeding of the 5,000 represented power over quantity, Jesus' walking on the Sea of Galilee in the middle of a stormy night represented power over natural law. This was not Jesus' resurrected body, which had the property of appearing and disappearing, but His truly human body as Mary's offspring. And Jesus enabled Peter to walk on water, too, as long as he kept his eyes on the Master. Matthew and Mark also record this miracle.

6. *The healing of the blind man (9:1–41)*. God has given us the ability to adapt to rather difficult circumstances, including the loss of body members. Most of us would rate the loss of sight as the ultimate affliction. In Jesus' day a blind person had no alternative to public charity. Correction! There *was* an alternative. Jesus provided it by healing the man born blind.

He who had known nothing but a life of helplessness found Someone who had power over helplessness. And physical sight was only one blessing. The healed man came to faith in the Son of God (9:35–38).

7. Raising Lazarus from the dead (11:1–44). Jesus' power over death was the climactic miracle of the seven that John selected. There could be no question as to Lazarus's deadness. The Jews of Bethany had been aware of his illness. They had been present four days previous when he was buried. Skeptics might try to argue that Jairus's daughter (Mark 5:22–24, 35–43) and the son of the widow of Nain (Luke 7:11–15) were not *really* dead, but there was no question about Lazarus.

In a spectacular demonstration of His deity, Jesus called Lazarus from the grave, and Lazarus came forth alive.

Jesus is the eternal I AM

When God called Moses to lead Israel out of Egypt, Moses said to God, " 'Suppose I go to the Israelites and say to them, "The God of your fathers has sent me to you," and they ask me, "What is his name?" Then what shall I tell them?'

"God said to Moses, 'I am who I am. This is what you are to say to the Israelites: "I AM has sent me to you" ' " (Exodus 3:13–14).

Jesus used that same emphatic expression of Himself: " 'Before Abraham was born, I am!' " (John 8:58). The meaning was not lost on the Jews who heard it. They recognized immediately that Jesus was claiming to be God.

Jesus made other claims:

" 'I am the bread of life' " (6:35).

" 'I am the light of the world' " (8:12; 9:5).

" 'I am the gate [door, King James Version]' " (10:7–9).

" 'I am the good shepherd' " (10:11, 14).

" 'I am the resurrection and the life' " (11:25).

" 'I am the way and the truth and the life' " (14:6).

" 'I am the true vine' " (15:1).

Public and private ministry

In broadest terms, John's gospel can be divided into Jesus' public ministry (the first 12 chapters), Jesus' private ministry to His disciples (chapters 13–17) and His death and resurrection (chapters 18–21).

In addition to Jesus' talks with His disciples, John records personal interviews Jesus had with the following:

Nicodemus, a Jewish ruler (3:1–21)

The Samaritan woman at Jacob's well (4:1–42)

The blind man (9:1–41)

Martha and Mary (11:1–46)

Pilate, the governor (18:33–38; 19:8–11)

Certainly some of the most significant teaching in the Gospel of John, not at all covered by Matthew, Mark and Luke, is Jesus' Upper Room discourse to His disciples (13:1—16:33). He announced to them His pending departure and promised to send the Holy Spirit in His stead to indwell them (14:17), to teach them (14:26), to empower them (15:26–27) and to guide them into all truth (16:13).

In His "high priestly prayer" (chapter 17), Jesus prays for His disciples and "'also for those who will believe in me through their message'" (17:20). It becomes clear from Jesus' prayer that He expects us to be fruitful Christians, and that He will give us the Holy Spirit to accomplish that fruitfulness and to unify us as His Body—the church—on earth.

Jesus' death and resurrection are the themes of chapters 18–20. Chapter 21 is an epilogue especially of interest because of Peter's reinstatement after his dismal failure in the court of the high priest (see John 18:15–18, 25–27).

John's Gospel ends, as do the other three, with the virtual conclusion of Jesus' earthly ministry. He had trained 12 disciples, one of whom had betrayed Him and left. None of the remaining 11 seems quite capable of following through in a ministry destined to make its impact in the succeeding 19 centuries in every corner of the earth. But Jesus knew what He was doing. He had not yet completed the equipping of these disciples. Indeed, the most important part of the equipping could not take place until after Jesus had ascended to heaven (see John 16:7, where Jesus speaks of the coming Counselor whom He would send).

In our next chapter we will see how that promise was fulfilled as we look at the New Testament's only history book and survey the birth of Jesus' church.

"Second mile" questions and topics

1. In John 15 Jesus compares Himself to a Palestine grapevine. God the Father is the "gardener"; Jesus' disciples, to whom the discourse is directed, are the branches of the vine. Find as many points of analogy as you can in this chapter between the grapevine and the lives of those related to Jesus as His "branches."

2. Read Jesus' prayer in John 17. List all the things Jesus asks in behalf of His followers. Is it reasonable that Jesus intends these benefits and blessings to be ours, too?

3

The Church Is Born
Acts

Into the Word Each Day

1.	Acts 1:6–14	The Holy Spirit is promised
2.	Acts 2:1–4, 32–33	The Holy Spirit comes
3.	Acts 7:54—8:3	Persecution
4.	Acts 9:1–6	The conversion of Saul [Paul]
5.	Acts 13:1–5	The first missionaries
6.	Acts 15:5–13, 19–20	Gentile rights
7.	Acts 27:27–44	Paul is shipwrecked

THE WRITER OF THE THIRD GOSPEL also wrote the Acts of the Apostles (compare Luke 1:1–3 with Acts 1:1–2). Luke obviously intended the two accounts to be companion volumes, the first covering the life and ministry of Jesus Christ while He was on earth, the second covering His life and ministry in the young church through the promised Holy Spirit whom He sent.

The full name—the Acts of the Apostles—is probably an addition to its original title, *Acts*, if indeed Luke gave it a title. The name is hardly appropriate. Only two of the apostles are mentioned in any depth—Peter and Paul. More properly, as many have pointed out, it is an account of the Acts of the Holy Spirit.

It begins as an immediate follow-up to the Gospel of Luke and ends with Paul preaching in Rome, capital of the empire. It spans an era of approximately 30 years, from A.D. 30 to A.D. 60, and probably was written in Rome while Luke was attending the aging Paul in his two years of house arrest (see Acts 28:30–31).

Acts is essentially the account of the ministry of Peter and Paul: Peter, the apostle to the Jews, and Paul, the apostle to the Gentiles. The midpoint (after chapter 12) where Luke lays down one story thread and takes up the other is a convenient two-part division of the book.

The only historical book

Acts is the only one of the New Testament books that was written as a history, although we are able to piece together other historical details of the early church by comments Paul and the other New Testament writers make. As a record of church history, Acts therefore occupies a very important place. It is the "hinge" between the four Gospels, with their accounts of the life and ministry of Jesus Christ, and the letters that follow, most of them written to church congregations and absorbed with teaching concerning the Christian life.

A reading of the final verses of Luke's Gospel and the opening verses of Luke's Acts will at once reveal the continuity. A key verse is found in the opening chapter: " 'You will receive power when the Holy Spirit comes on you; and you will be my witnesses in Jerusalem, and in all Judea and Samaria, and to the ends of the earth' " (1:8). The promised Holy Spirit would soon be descending on Jesus' followers, giving birth to the church and empowering that church to fulfill Jesus' commission to make disciples in all the world.

Notice the radiations: Jerusalem, Judea, Samaria, the ends of the earth. We will see how remarkably that prophecy was fulfilled in the 30-year span covered by this book. And of course the church continued to thrive spiritually and expand geographically during the first three centuries of the Christian era despite (or, more properly, because of) intense persecution.

A successor for Judas

After witnessing the ascent of Jesus Christ to heaven (Acts 1:9), the apostles returned to the upstairs room in Jerusalem where they had been staying. We are told that the total company numbered "about a hundred and twenty" (1:15).

Peter, still assuming the role of spokesman for the group, announced an election to replace Judas Iscariot, the disciple who had committed suicide after betraying Jesus. There are some who insist the procedure was in order. Others believe it was another case of Peter's impetuosity outrunning the divine will; that Paul, who does not surface in the book of Acts until 7:58, was the man God had in mind to complete the apostolate.

In any case, the disciple-leaders proposed two names—Joseph Barsabbas and Matthias—and from that narrow field of close followers of Jesus the lot fell to Matthias and he "was added to the eleven apostles" (1:26).

Pentecost

Pentecost was the second of three great annual festivals decreed by Jehovah for ancient Israel to keep. The name means fiftieth, and it occurred 50 days after Passover (Leviticus 23:15–16). It was a harvest festival, occurring at the height of the grain harvest, and therefore it was a time to rejoice in the fruitfulness God had granted His people.

The festival swelled Jerusalem with pilgrims, who traveled

from all points of the Empire to be present for this important feast. And into that scene, on that precise day, there was "suddenly a sound like the blowing of a violent wind." It "filled the whole house where they [the 120] were sitting. They saw what seemed to be tongues of fire that separated and came to rest on each of them. All of them were filled with the Holy Spirit and began to speak in other tongues as the Spirit enabled them" (2:2–4).

If the 120 were astonished, the Jerusalem populace was more so. Here were common Galileans speaking the languages of " 'Parthians, Medes and Elamites, residents of Mesopotamia, Judea and Cappadocia, Pontus and Asia, Phrygia and Pamphylia, Egypt and the parts of Libya near Cyrene.' " Visitors from Rome, Cretans, Arabs—all heard these men and women " 'declaring the wonders of God' " in languages intelligible to them (2:9–11).

Peter, full of the Holy Spirit, seized the initiative. His address began with Joel's Old Testament prediction of this very event (Joel 2:28–32; Acts 2:17–21), and followed with a clear-cut witness to " 'Jesus of Nazareth,' " whose miracles were well-known. " 'You, with the help of wicked men, put him to death by nailing him to the cross,' " Peter says accusingly. " 'But God raised him from the dead, freeing him from the agony of death, because it was impossible for death to keep its hold on him' " (2:23–24).

Jesus, however, did not remain dead. " 'He was not abandoned to the grave, nor did his body see decay. God has raised this Jesus to life, and we are all witnesses of the fact. Exalted to the right hand of God, he has received from the Father the promised Holy Spirit and has poured out what you now see and hear' " (2:31–33).

Peter's conclusion: " 'God has made this Jesus, whom you crucified, both Lord and Christ' " (2:36). And his application: " 'Repent and be baptized, every one of you, in the name of Jesus Christ so that your sins may be forgiven. And you will receive the gift of the Holy Spirit'" (2:38).

Note well the core message of that day of Pentecost sermon —the death for mankind's sins, the resurrection and exaltation of Jesus. It was the undeviating theme of all Peter's preaching, whether to the populace as a whole on the day of Pentecost, the Jewish Council (4:10–12; 5:30–31) or to the Gentile Cornelius (10:39–43). It was the message Paul preached in Pisidian Antioch (13:26–39) and even to the Athenians (17:30–31), where Paul presses for repentance on the basis of Christ's resurrection from the dead.

These apostles had but one message to give to the world. It was a message of redemption accomplished by Christ Jesus through His death, resurrection and exaltation.

Converts—and persecution

The Scriptures inform us that 3,000 people turned to Christ as a result of Peter's sermon on the day of Pentecost (Acts 2:41). These Christians became a closely knit community (2:42–47) to which new converts were added daily.

But resistance soon developed. First it was the "priests and the captain of the temple guard and the Sadducees" (4:1) who jailed Peter and John overnight (4:3) and "commanded them not to speak or teach at all in the name of Jesus" (4:18). Those threats failing, the "high priest and all his associates . . . arrested the apostles and put them in the public jail" (5:17–18). This time an angel of the Lord freed them, instructing them, "'Go, stand in the temple courts . . . and tell the people the full message of this new life'" (5:20).

Stephen, "a man full of faith and of the Holy Spirit" (6:5), became the first Christian martyr, being stoned to death for his eloquent but accusing sermon (7:1–60).

Stephen's martyrdom triggered a veritable eruption of per-

secution that forced all but the apostles from Jerusalem (8:1).
But wherever the Christians went, in Judea and Samaria (remember Jesus' prediction that they were to be witnesses in Judea and Samaria?), they "preached the word" (8:4; 11:19), thus further spreading the good news of Jesus Christ.

Saul (later named Paul), a relatively young Pharisee who had been present at Stephen's death, became a leader in the persecution (9:1–2).

James, brother of John, was the first of the apostles to be put to death (12:1–2). King Herod probably would have subjected Peter to the same fate had not an angel miraculously liberated him from the maximum security cell where he was being held (12:3–10).

It was a persecution sometimes mild, sometimes intense, that was to hound the young church for the first three centuries of its existence.

The church reaches the Gentiles

The church, up to this point, had been almost exclusively a Jewish phenomenon. Much of its beginning activity was in the Temple—until the Temple leaders made the Christians unwelcome. To have turned from the observances of their fathers would have been repugnant to any Jew—even a Christian Jew.

The spread of the gospel into Samaria (8:4 ff.) through the ministry of Philip, did not represent a radical departure from the Jewish milieu, for the Samaritans were part Jewish. And the Ethiopian treasurer whom Philip met and converted to Christ on the Gaza road (8:26 ff.) was evidently a Jewish proselyte, for he "had gone to Jerusalem to worship" (8:27) and was engrossed in "reading the book of Isaiah the prophet" (8:28) when Philip joined his chariot.

Cornelius (10:1 ff.), however, represented a departure. Cornelius and his family, although "devout and God-fearing," were Gentiles. God had to do some persuading before Peter was mentally ready to minister the gospel to Cornelius (see 10:9–20, 27–28).

But at the home of Cornelius it was a repetition of the day of Pentecost. The Holy Spirit descended on the assembled, waiting group, and the Jews who had accompanied Peter "heard them speaking in tongues [*other languages* is an alternate translation] and praising God" (10:46). On the spot Peter baptized Cornelius and his household.

The door to the Gentiles had been pushed open just a crack. Meanwhile, it was being opened a bit wider at Antioch, where believers from Cyprus and Cyrene "began to speak to Greeks also, telling them the good news about the Lord Jesus" (11:20).

But it was Paul, the apostle to the Gentiles, who really swung the door wide open. In a lifetime of ministry that took him throughout Asia Minor, Greece, Italy and possibly Spain, Paul fulfilled the evangelistic mandate given to him at his conversion near Damascus to "'carry [Christ's] name before the Gentiles and their kings'" (9:15).

Paul (his name was changed from Saul to Paul) made three missionary journeys. The first, undertaken with Barnabas, covered Cyprus and a small part of Asia Minor. The second, in the company of Silas, took the team overland through Asia Minor and ultimately into Greece, where successful churches were established at Philippi, Thessalonica, Corinth and other communities.

The third journey (Acts 18:23 ff.) largely retraced the route of the second. Paul's purpose was to strengthen the disciples he had made previously.

As Gentiles came into the church, a major issue developed. The Jewish believers, as we have noted, kept the Old Testament Law and observed Jewish feasts and holy days. What about the Gentiles? Was it necessary for them to do the same?

The Jerusalem Council (Acts 15:1–29), the first such conference to be held, convened to decide this important and potentially divisive issue. Paul and Barnabas, just back from their first mission, were strongly on the side of freeing Gentiles from the encumbering Law. Peter, who had been God's instrument for the conversion of Cornelius, was on that side of the issue, too. Peter spoke (15:7–11). Paul and Barnabas spoke (15:12).

The ensuing decision, worded by James, was based not only on the testimony of those who had debated the issue but on a clear scriptural precedent (Amos 9:11–12). James said, "'We should not make it difficult for the Gentiles who are turning to God. Instead we should write to them, telling them to abstain from food polluted by idols, from sexual immorality, from the meat of strangled animals and from blood'" (15:19–21).

It was a landmark decision. It eventually would free the Christian church to develop without the constraints of the Jewish faith. It influenced the whole course of church history.

Paul's closing years

But the mixing of Jew with Gentile was intolerable to many Jews. They plagued Paul, and their protests hindered his evangelistic ministry. Back in Jerusalem after his third missionary journey, Paul ran head-on into some of these "Judaizers," who came within a handbreadth of killing him.

Taken into Roman custody, mainly for his own protection, Paul had opportunity to speak to kings and governors (24:9–21, 24–26; 25:8–12, 23; 26:1–29). His appeal to Caesar (25:10–11) ultimately took him to Rome. The story of his being shipwrecked enroute (Acts 27) is one of the more suspenseful passages in the Bible.

Luke closes his account with Paul under house arrest in Rome. Tradition, with some between-the-lines support from certain of Paul's letters, has it that Paul was ultimately released, that he made the trip into Spain that he had hoped to make (Romans 15:24, 28), and was later imprisoned a second time in Rome and executed. But this we do not know for certain.

Clement, an early church father, said, "Paul . . . taught righteousness to all the world, and when he had reached the limits of the West he gave his testimony before the rulers and then passed from the world and was taken up into the Holy Place."

Recapitulation

Luke, who begins Acts with a group of uncertain apostles on a mountain outside Jerusalem, ends it 30 years later with the Christian church well established throughout the Roman Empire.

Jesus, who had said, "'You will be my witnesses'" (Acts 1:8), empowered these early Christians to be exactly that. They witnessed enthusiastically, unashamedly, in season and out.

A consecutive reading of all of Acts uncovers some place names that we will encounter elsewhere in the New Testament: Philippi (16:12), Thessalonica (17:1), Corinth (18:1), Ephesus (19:1). They are places where Paul and his associates planted Christian churches. And Paul, never content to evangelize and leave, used the vehicle of letter-writing to keep in touch with these churches and to continue his teaching of them.

It is to these letters and their contents that we next turn in this survey of the New Testament.

"Second mile" questions and topics

1. Note Acts 4:32–35, where the early believers in Jerusalem sold their possessions and pooled the money, living evidently communally—a system neither advocated nor apparently practiced elsewhere in the New Testament or in New Testament times. Read Acts 8:1–4 and see if you can find one possible reason why the Holy Spirit would have guided the Jerusalem Christians to sell their possessions.

2. In Acts 9 we have the first account of Paul's conversion. In Acts 22 Paul relates his conversion experience to the mob in Jerusalem who wanted to kill him. In Acts 26 he repeats his testimony in Caesarea before King Agrippa. What three things did God specifically appoint Paul to do, according to Acts 26:17–18? What two things were to be the result?

4

Paul's Gospel Explained
Romans

Into the Word Each Day

1. Romans 1:1–4, 11–17 The gospel Paul preached
2. Romans 3:21–30 Justification is by faith
3. Romans 5:1–8 Peace with God
4. Romans 8:22–31 God works for good
5. Romans 10:1–10 Paul's desire for the Jews
6. Romans 12:9–21 Love must be sincere
7. Romans 13:1–7 Submit to government

THUS FAR WE HAVE LOOKED AT the four Gospels, with their records of Jesus' life in the flesh, and the Acts, which continues the chronological account of how Jesus' apostles, Spirit-filled, perpetuated not only His message but His very life, until members of His Body, the Church, could be found in most of the Roman world.

With Acts behind us, we have concluded the historical part of the New Testament. Although, as we said, there are references in many of the New Testament letters that help us to fill out our knowledge of first century church history, the purpose of the letters is not primarily to give us more historical detail.

The purpose of the letters

The primary purpose of these letters is to convey Christian teaching. The writers seek to translate the message of Christ, as they received it, into practical terms for day-to-day living.

Some of the letters are long and detailed, some are very short. They are written either to Christian churches or to individual Christians. A few were written to counter error that had crept into the church. Romans—the letter we will be looking at in this chapter—is a presentation of Christian doctrine. The two Corinthian letters were written to correct abuses in the church at Corinth. The Thessalonian letters deal especially with matters concerning Jesus' predicted return to earth. Hebrews, as the name suggests, is concerned with bridging the gap between Old Testament Law and ritual and New Testament Christian faith. Each, as we shall see, had its special purpose.

Revelation, the final letter, if it can be so categorized, was written to a block of seven churches in Asia Minor. Not only is there a specific message for each of these seven churches, but the inspired writer goes on to outline what will take place in the future in relation to Christ's return.

If we were to be treating the New Testament letters from a strictly chronological standpoint (a somewhat arbitrary attempt at best), we would first look at First and Second Thessalonians, in all probability Paul's earliest letters and possibly the earliest of any of the New Testament Scriptures. Since the dates of the writing of some of these letters are only approximate, we will follow the order in which the books appear in your New Testament.

We turn, therefore, first to Romans.

A doctrinal statement

Of all the New Testament books, Paul's letter to the Romans is the most systematic in its presentation of Christian teaching. It was written probably in A.D. 55 or 56 to a church the apostle had not yet visited. Quite possibly Paul was in Corinth on his third mission when he wrote it, perhaps sending it in the care of Phoebe of Cenchrea, who was about to visit Rome and whom Paul commends to the Roman believers (Romans 16:1–2).

Redemption is the general theme of Romans, the key verses being 3:23–24: "All have sinned and fall short of the glory of God, and are justified freely by his grace through the redemption that came by Christ Jesus."

Paul begins with a short introduction characteristic of all his letters. Our style today is to put our signature at the end of our letters. In the first century, writers employed a more sensible style and announced who they were at the beginning of their letters.

Paul gets the theme of the gospel of God into the forefront of his long first sentence, and never lets it rest. For Paul as for the evangelists Matthew, Mark, Luke and John, the gospel or good news is linked to God's Son, Jesus Christ, the human descendant of King David, but equally the divine Son of God, as His resurrection from the dead attested (1:3–4).

Paul concludes his introduction with one of the most familiar statements in Romans: "I am not ashamed of the gospel, because it is the power of God for the salvation of everyone who believes: first for the Jew, then for the Gentile. For in the gospel a righteousness from God is revealed, a righteousness that is by faith from first to last, just as it is written: 'The righteous will live by faith'" (1:16–17).

Universal guilt: all have sinned

In his systematic way Paul begins by proving that all have sinned and therefore stand guilty before God. Even those who have not had specific Bible teaching have failed to acknowledge God's "invisible qualities—his eternal power and divine nature" (1:20) that can be deduced from nature around us. Consequently, Paul says, "men are without excuse."

Because people have refused to respond to what God has revealed of Himself, "God gave them over" to sexual sin (1:24), to "shameful lusts" (1:26), to a "depraved mind" (1:28). The morbid litany of sin that ensues is only too familiar in our world today. God does not necessarily choose to strike with a bolt of lightning all who deliberately sin; He rather gives them over to their own perverted desires until they have "received in themselves the due penalty for their perversion" (1:27).

Yet the Jew (here Paul addresses especially the believers of Jewish background) dares not sit in judgment on Gentile sinners, for Jews are equally guilty; they "do the same things" (2:1). Paul very carefully proves both Gentile and Jew guilty before God, and declares that "all who sin apart from the [Old Testament] law will also perish apart from the law, and all who sin under the law [that is, the Jews] will be judged by the law" (2:12).

The condemning conclusion: "Jews and Gentiles alike are all under sin" (3:9).

Justification: the provision of redemption

But into that very predicament came Jesus Christ, God's own Son, testified to by the Law and the Prophets—two major sections of the Old Testament of the Bible. "God presented him [Jesus] as a sacrifice of atonement, through faith in His blood. He did this to . . . demonstrate his justice at the present time, so as to be just and the one who justifies the man who has faith in Jesus" (3:25–26).

To prove that this righteousness through Christ is not something we work for and earn, Paul cites Abraham, forefather of the Jewish religion, and notes that the Old Testament Scriptures affirm that " 'Abraham believed God, and it was credited to him as righteousness' " (4:3, quoting Genesis 15:6). Righteousness, the forgiveness of our sins, is therefore not something we earn and deserve, but something received as a free gift by faith. "To the man who does not work but trusts God who justifies the wicked, his faith is credited as righteousness" (4:5).

Those who have reached out in faith to this redemption provided by God through Jesus Christ

- have peace with God (5:1)
- rejoice in the hope of the glory of God (5:2)
- rejoice in our sufferings (5:3), knowing the "suffering produces perseverance; perseverance, character; and character, hope" that does not disappoint us "because God has poured out his love into our hearts by the Holy Spirit, whom he has given us" (5:5)
- will be saved from God's wrath (5:9)
- "rejoice in God through our Lord Jesus Christ, through whom we have now received reconciliation" (5:11)

Sanctification: the effect of redemption

Chapter 6 of Romans brings another change of emphasis. Paul has concluded that all have sinned and stand condemned. He has pointed out the remedy for the sinner: justification through the sacrifice of God's Son, Jesus Christ, accepted by faith. But being in a right standing with God is not the whole answer.

The believer does not get very far into his new standing before he realizes that a tug-of-war is at work within him. The old life of sin that was the root of all his spiritual trouble is still very much alive and is determined that he will not live a life of righteousness. Paul describes this tug-of-war in chapter 7: "What I want to do I do not do, but what I hate I do. I have the desire to do what is good, but I cannot carry it out. For what I do is not the good I want to do; no, the evil I do not want to do—this I keep on doing" (7:15–19).

The apostle points to the culprit: "If I do what I do not want to do, it is no longer I who do it, but it is sin living in me that does it" (7:20). His summary: "In my inner being I delight in God's law; but I see another law at work in the members of my body, waging war against the law of my mind and making me a prisoner of the law of sin at work within my members. . . . So then, I myself in my mind am a slave to God's law, but in the sinful nature a slave to the law of sin" (7:23–25).

What is the solution to this seeming impasse? "Nothing good lives in me," Paul admits, "that is, in my sinful nature" (7:18). And therein is the key to deliverance. Paul reminds us that this Jesus, with whom we are identified, died and rose again. The very act of baptism is symbolic of that identification: "Don't you know that all of us who were baptized into Christ Jesus were baptized into his death?" (6:3).

But the symbolism goes farther, Paul says. "We were therefore buried with him through baptism into death in order that, just as Christ was raised from the dead through the glory of the Father, we too may live a new life" (6:4). Jesus did not stay in the grave; He arose to a new level of physical life and eventually to ascend to God the Father and take His place at the Father's right hand. And our identification with Jesus Christ covers that resurrection and ascension as well: "If we have been united with him in his death, we will certainly also be united with him in his resurrection" (6:5).

What is the practical consequence of all this? Paul says it is freedom from sin. "We know that our old self [the one giving us all the trouble] was crucified with him so that the body of sin might be rendered powerless, that we should no longer be slaves to sin—because anyone who has died has been freed from sin" (6:6–7).

We are therefore to "count [ourselves] dead to sin but alive to God in Christ Jesus" (6:11). We are not to "let sin reign in [our] mortal bod[ies] so that [we] obey its evil desires" (6:12). We are not to "offer the parts of [our] bod[ies] to sin, as instruments of wickedness."

We are to "offer [ourselves] to God, as those who have been brought from death to life; and offer the parts of [our] bod[ies] to him as instruments of righteousness" (6:13).

And what is the result of this total yielding of ourselves to God? God fills us with His Spirit. He will possess only what we yield to Him. When we yield everything, He fills us.

Paul outlines some benefits of the Spirit-filled life in chapter 8:

    no condemnation (8:1)
    freedom from the law of sin and death (8:2)
    life and peace (8:6)
    "life" for our mortal bodies (8:11)
    sonship—and daughtership—with God (8:15)
    co-heirship with Christ (8:17)
    the ultimate redemption of our bodies (8:23)
    assistance in prayer (8:26–27)
    conformity to Jesus Christ (8:29)

Paul bursts into some of the most exalted prose of the New Testament as he contemplates this great theme: "What, then, shall we say in response to this? If God is for us, who can be against us? He who did not spare his own Son, but gave him up for us all—how will he not also, along with him, graciously give us all things? . . . Who shall separate us from the love of Christ? . . . I am convinced that neither death nor life, neither angels nor demons, neither the present nor the future, nor any powers, neither height nor depth, nor anything else in all creation, will be able to separate us from the love of God that is in Christ Jesus our Lord."

Jew and Gentile: the scope of redemption

Again there is a distinct change of theme in Paul's letter. He shares his burden for his own race, the Jews. As we noted in the last chapter, the church at first was comprised entirely of Jews and proselytes who turned to Christ by the thousands (Acts 2:41; 4:4; 6:7). But Jewish religious leaders, who from the first were antagonistic to this new Messiah (see John 7:47–48), initiated a widespread persecution of Jerusalem Christians (Acts 8:1).

Gentile converts served further to polarize Judaism and Christianity. The decision of the first church council that Gentile Christians need not keep Jewish Law, necessary for the growth of the church among Gentiles, nevertheless alienated many of the Jews.

Paul regrets deeply this alienation. "I could wish that I myself were cursed and cut off from Christ for the sake of my brothers, those of my own race, the people of Israel," he says (9:3–4). "Brothers, my heart's desire and prayer to God for the Israelites is that they may be saved" (10:1).

But Paul sees ultimate national salvation for his people. "Did God reject his people? By no means! . . . God did not reject his people, whom he foreknew" (11:1–2). Rather, their alienation was in order that Gentiles might be saved: "Israel has experienced a hardening in part until the full number of the Gentiles has come in" (11:25).

God who called Abraham to father the Jewish nation and

who declared His everlasting love to His people, has not re-
neged on His commitment. "All Israel will be saved," Paul
affirms, "as it is written:

> 'The deliverer will come from Zion;
>   he will turn godlessness away from Jacob.
> And this is my covenant with them
>   when I take away their sins'"
>
> Romans 11:26–27.

Service: the fruit of redemption

Paul always follows teaching with practical admonition,
and his letter to the Romans is no exception. Note the "therefore" that begins this section: "Therefore I urge you, brothers,
in view of God's mercy, to offer your bodies as living sacrifices, holy and pleasing to God—which is your spiritual worship. Do not conform any longer to the pattern of this world,
but be transformed by the renewing of your mind. Then you
will be able to test and approve what God's will is—his good,
pleasing and perfect will" (12:1–2).

As he will remark to the Corinthian church and to the
Ephesian church, he regards the believers in Rome as a body—
Christ's body. "In Christ we who are many form one body,
and each member belongs to all the others. We have different
gifts, according to the grace given us" (12:5–6). We should
exercise these gifts by faith for the good of the body. Above
all, we should love one another sincerely (12:9–10). As believers we are to be zealous, joyful, patient, faithful in prayer
(12:11–12). We are to share with fellow-believers in need and
practice hospitality (12:13).

Our behavior should be characterized by meekness, em-
pathy, harmony, humility, non-retaliation, good works (12:
17–21).

In his only reference to the Christian and civil government, Paul urges submission to "the governing authorities" (13:1). His reason: he sees government as "established by God" (13:2). Therefore he who "rebels against the authority is rebelling against what God has instituted" (13:2). Significantly, neither in the Acts nor in any reference in Paul's 13 or 14 letters is there an instance of his disobeying civil authorities. Paul practiced what he preached.

Chapter 14 and the first part of chapter 15 are concerned with "him whose faith is weak" (14:1) and our obligation to not offend these weaker Christians. "Let us stop passing judgment on one another," Paul says. "Instead, make up your mind not to put any stumbling block or obstacle in your brother's way" (14:13).

Paul's conclusion

In a long conclusion, beginning with 15:14, Paul refers again to his commission as an apostle to the Gentiles (15:15–16), and to his missionary ministry (15:19–20). He looks forward to visiting Rome on his way to Spain (15:23–24), and mentions his immediate task of taking to Jerusalem "a contribution for the poor among the saints in Jerusalem" donated by Christians in "Macedonia and Achaia" (15:25–26).

Paul implies (16:1) that he is sending this letter to them by "a servant of the church in Cenchrea"—Phoebe, whom he hopes they will receive "in a way worthy of the saints" (16:1–2). He conveys greetings to a long list of friends and associates (16:3–16) and in turn conveys the greetings of Timothy (16:21), Tertius (16:22), Gaius (16:23), Erastus and Quartus (16:23).

After an exhortation to unity (6:19–20), Paul closes with a benediction that summarizes his letter—a benediction especially appropriate to the Roman Christians:

"Now to him who is able to establish you by my gospel and
the proclamation of Jesus Christ, according to the revelation
of the mystery hidden for long ages past, but now revealed
and made known through the prophetic writings by the command of the eternal God, so that all nations might believe and
obey him—to the only wise God be glory forever through
Jesus Christ! Amen" (16:25–27).

"Second mile" questions and topics

1. Examine Romans 1:24–32. If the three paragraphs spell
out a progressively intensifying rebellion against God, are
you surprised by some of the things you find in the third and
ultimate category (1:28–31)? Note 1:26–27. What does this say
concerning the popular view that homosexuality is something a person cannot help?

2. A frequently quoted Bible verse is Romans 8:28. But it
has to be seen in its context. Study Romans 8:26–29. What is
God's desire for us (8:29)? How is this desire accomplished
(8:26–27)? What, then, are the believers' responsibilities in
order for God "in all things" to work "for the good of those
. . . called according to his purpose"?

Letters to an Immature Church
First and Second Corinthians

Into the Word Each Day

1. 1 Corinthians 1:18–24   The message of the cross
2. 1 Corinthians 6:12–20   Honor God with your body
3. 1 Corinthians 11:23–29   The Lord's Supper
4. 1 Corinthians 13   Love
5. 1 Corinthians 15:51–58   "I tell you a mystery"
6. 2 Corinthians 5:17—6:2   Christ's ambassadors
7. 2 Corinthians 9:6–11   The grace of giving

CORINTH, THE MOST SPLENDID commercial city of Greece, was situated on the narrow stem of land connecting central Greece with the Peloponnesus, a section of land stretching out into the Mediterranean Sea. Navigation around the Peloponnesus was a risky, two-hundred-mile trip. Sea captains preferred to let their vessels be dragged on rollers across the five-mile isthmus. And that is how land-locked Corinth became internationally famous as a shipping and trading center.

The city of 500,000 people was distinctively cosmopolitan, and the presence of large numbers of sailors served to intensify its bent toward lust and immorality. It had the reputation of being one of the most profligate and corrupt cities in the whole Roman Empire.

Yet Corinth was a proud city. It had had an illustrious past. It was famous for its Corinthian bronze and Corinthian pottery. Rebuilt by Julius Caesar in 46 B.C., it became the capital of Achaia.

Dominating the center of the city was the marketplace, richly colonnaded and embellished with monuments. A subterranean channel furnished cold water to the shops fronting the marketplace, an area referred to by Paul in First Corinthians 10:25. A Roman basilica and Apollo's Temple were other landmarks in a city that boasted a theater capable of seating 18,000.

Paul founded the Corinthian church

The crowning achievement of Paul's second missionary journey was the Christian church he founded in Corinth. (For details, see Acts 18:1–18.) In a year and a half, assisted by a Jew named Aquila and his wife, Priscilla, the apostle brought to birth a major church. Apollos followed Paul at Corinth (Acts 18:27–28), greatly helping the growth of the church. There were Jews among its members and *some* people of means ("not many"), but most were poor, unlearned converts from paganism (see 1 Corinthians 1:26; 12:2).

Paul wrote at least three letters to the Corinthian church. The first, which he alludes to in First Corinthians 5:9, has been lost to us. There is no valid foundation for assuming, as some scholars do, that Paul's earlier letter is a part of our present First Corinthians.

Paul wrote First Corinthians in response to a letter from the church asking him certain questions (7:1), and partly, too, in response to word that had reached him concerning existing troubles in the Corinthian church (1:11; 16:17). First Corinthians was written probably in the spring of A.D. 56 during Paul's stay in Ephesus. At that time the Corinthian church would have been scarcely more than five years old.

Like Romans, which we looked at in our last chapter, First Corinthians begins with a brief introduction. Paul salutes "the church of God in Corinth" (1:2), offers a benediction (1:3), thanks God for the grace the believers have been given "in Christ Jesus" (1:4), and expresses his confidence that the faithful God "will keep [them] strong to the end, so that [they] will be blameless on the day of our Lord Jesus Christ" (1:8).

Problem one: factions

Despite such words of praise, the apostle wastes no time in getting to the first of 10 distinct problems that he addresses. He had been informed by "some from Chloe's household" (1:11) that the members were quarreling. They had lined up behind Paul, behind Apollos, behind Peter (Cephas) and—some of the holier-than-thou types—behind Christ.

Paul attacks the problem frontally in 3:1–6. It is God who counts—not His human messengers such as Apollos or Paul. Paul may have planted the seed and Apollos may have watered it, but it is God who makes it grow. Ultimately the Corinthians are responsible to God (3:9).

A "Day" is coming, a Day of judgment, when fire "will test the quality of each man's work" (3:13). Therefore, "no more boasting about men!" (3:21).

Problem two: sexual immorality

As if the factions were not bad enough, the church had allowed a man practicing incest to remain a member (5:1). Paul moves swiftly to deal with such a person: "Hand this man over to Satan, so that the sinful nature may be destroyed and his spirit saved on the day of the Lord" (5:5), and,

"'Expel the wicked man from among you'" (5:13), a procedure several times urged by Moses for Israel in cases of immorality (see Deuteronomy 17:7; 19:19; 22:21, 24; 24:7).

Problem three: lawsuits

The litany of disappointing behavior continues. Brother is taking brother to court (6:1). Paul says, "The very fact that you have lawsuits among you means you have been completely defeated already. Why not rather be wronged? Why not rather be cheated?" (6:7).

Paul's solution: an arbitrator within the church. "Is it possible that there is nobody among you wise enough to judge a dispute between believers?" (6:5).

Problem four: more sexual immorality

There seem to have been more instances of sexual immorality than just the man guilty of incest. Paul devotes another whole section to the subject (6:12–20).

Freedom in Christ does not mean freedom to be promiscuous. "The body is not meant for sexual immorality, but for the Lord, and the Lord for the body" (6:13). "Flee from sexual immorality. . . . Do you not know that your body is a temple of the Holy Spirit? . . . Therefore honor God with your body" (6:18–20).

Problem five: marital relationships

Paul now comes to the matters the church wrote him about. The first concerns whether Christians ought to get married and to give their children in marriage (7:1).

Yes, says Paul, with some personal reservations. "Since there is so much immorality, each man should have his own wife, and each woman her own husband. The husband should fulfill his marital duty to his wife, and likewise the wife to her husband" (7:2–3).

Yet Paul says all this "as a concession, not as a command" (7:6). He makes it quite clear that for the unattached "it is good for them to stay unmarried, as I am" (7:8).

But those already married should not separate. "A wife must not separate from her husband. But if she does, she must remain unmarried or else be reconciled to her husband. And a husband must not divorce his wife" (7:10–11). This rule applies even if the other partner is an unbeliever (7:12–13).

Paul's preference for the single state stems from two considerations: (1) "The time is short" (7:29). The Lord could return soon. (2) The unmarried are freer to devote themselves to the Lord's work (7:32–35).

Problem six: food sacrificed to idols

In a predominantly pagan city like Corinth, Christians had a problem. Any meat they bought in the public marketplace in all probability had been first offered to idols. Was it right for Christians to eat such meat?

(Note, incidentally, that the rightness or wrongness of eating meat is not the issue. In fact, the strong implication is that meat-eating is normal for the believer, as for the unbeliever.)

The issue concerning eating meat first offered to idols hinges on what it does to the person with a "weak conscience" (8:9–10). Idols are nothing, and there is but one God (8:4). But there may be fellow Christians who see in these idols the demons behind them (10:20). We must respect their consciences.

What if you are invited to a meal? "Eat whatever is put before you without raising questions of conscience," Paul answers (10:27). But if anyone specifically says that the meat has been offered in sacrifice, then "do not eat it, both for the sake of the man who told you and for conscience' sake—the other man's conscience" (10:28).

Conclusion: "Whether you eat or drink or whatever you do, do it all for the glory of God. Do not cause anyone to stumble, whether Jews, Greeks or the church of God" (10:31–32).

Problem seven: propriety in worship

Not only is the woman to pray and prophesy with covered head (11:5) to indicate that she "is the glory of man" (11:7) and comes "from man" (11:8), but in the partaking of the Lord's Supper there is to be order and deference to others (11:17–34) as this solemn and emblematic ordinance is regularly repeated. "Whoever eats the bread or drinks the cup of the Lord in an unworthy manner will be guilty of sinning against the body and blood of the Lord" (11:27).

Problem eight: misuse of spiritual gifts

God has given spiritual gifts to His Church. They are of different kinds (12:4), but they are given for the common good (12:7)—given "to each man [literal 'to each one'], just as he [the Spirit] determines" (12:11). Their ultimate purpose is the building up of the church (14:12).

Paul employs the analogy of the human body. Just as one body has many parts, so does the "body of Christ," of which each of the Corinthian believers is a part (12:27). There is an order of importance to the gifts—"first of all apostles, second prophets, third teachers, then workers of miracles, also those having gifts of healing, those able to help others, those with gifts of administration, and those speaking in different kinds of tongues" (12:28–29). The diversity is important to the functioning of the body (12:21), and in fact some of the weaker, less prominent parts are indispensable and get treated with special honor (12:22–23).

The issue of the gift of tongues and the interpretation of tongues was a special problem in the Corinthian church, and Paul takes some pains to show the limited application of this gift to the church in corporate worship (12:2, 14–18) and evangelism (14:22–23). He urges the Corinthians to "desire . . . especially the gift of prophecy" (14:1, 5). As with the Lord's Supper, "everything should be done in a fitting and orderly way" (14:40).

But things should also be done in love. The tongues may be angelic, the prophecy may fathom all mysteries, the faith may move mountains, the giving may be to the point of martyrdom, but if the gifts are exercised without love, we are resounding gongs and clanging cymbals; we are nothing at all (13:1–3). Paul's short but comprehensive statement on love (13:1–13) is one of the New Testament's crown gems.

Problem nine: questions concerning resurrection

Certain members of the Corinthian church were evidently doubting that believers who died would be resurrected (15:12). Paul reminds them that a cardinal point of the earliest gospel witness is that Jesus "was raised on the third day according to the Scriptures" (15:4). He argues that "if there is no resurrection of the dead, then not even Christ has been raised" (15:13). And if Christ has not been raised, Paul's preaching and their faith have been useless (15:14).

But Paul comes quickly to the point: "Christ has indeed been raised from the dead, the firstfruits of those who have fallen asleep" (15:20).

"How are the dead raised? With what kind of body will they come?" (15:35). Resurrection is analogous to a planted seed, Paul says. The seed buried in the ground bears little resemblance to the green shoot that springs up as warmth and moisture revitalize it. So the resurrected body. It will be "as [God] has determined" (15:38). But it will be "imperishable," glorious, powerful, spiritual (15:42–44).

Paul concludes his discussion of resurrection with some practical admonition: "Therefore, my dear brothers, stand firm. Let nothing move you. Always give yourselves fully to the work of the Lord, because you know that your labor in the Lord is not in vain" (15:58).

Problem ten: questions about monetary giving

The last problem Paul deals with is one he treats in greater detail in Second Corinthians. With no church buildings to pay for and keep up, with no pastors to support, with the missionary team (Paul and company) by choice self-supporting (see Acts 20:33–34), there was less need for the kind of financial backing so important to today's church. But Christians in Jerusalem, economically depressed, were suffering, and Paul was anxious to convey a generous offering to them to meet their temporal necessities.

Paul instructs each Corinthian believer
> to set aside a sum of money in keeping with his income
> to do it the first day of the week
> to save it up against Paul's coming for it (16:2)

The letter concludes with personal requests, final greetings and a benediction.

Second Corinthians

Paul's second preserved letter to the Corinthian church was written from somewhere in Macedonia, probably during the summer of A.D. 56. He had learned from Titus that the first letter had provoked repentance on the part of some (2 Corinthians 2:6–8), but that Jewish Christians (11:22), teaching strict adherence to the Old Testament Law, had maligned Paul's deportment (10:2) and discounted his person (10:10). Paul proceeds to defend his ministry (1:8—7:16) and his apostleship (11:1—13:10).

Sandwiched between these two themes is the long and important passage on financial support we mentioned earlier. Interspersed throughout the letter are other rich veins of spiritual truth.

Paul defends his ministry

Alluding to his sufferings (1:8–10; 4:8–10) as a minister of Jesus Christ, Paul calls the Corinthians his "letter" of reference (3:1–3), commending him and his ministry for all to see. He talks about his ministry: "We do not use deception, nor do we distort the word of God. On the contrary, by setting forth the truth plainly we commend ourselves to every man's conscience in the sight of God" (4:2). He says, "We make it our goal to please [the Lord]" (5:9), bearing in mind that "we must all appear before the judgment seat of Christ, that each one may receive what is due him for the things done while in the body, whether good or bad" (5:10).

Paul defends his apostleship

As to his apostleship, Paul reminds the Corinthians that "the things that mark an apostle—signs, wonders and miracles— were done among [them] with great perseverance" (12:12). He calls the troublemakers "false apostles, deceitful workmen" (11:13) who have sought to lead astray the Corinthians from their "sincere and pure devotion to Christ" (11:3) with a "different gospel" (11:4).

He bares the details of some of his sufferings as an apostle

(11:23–29, cf. 6:4–10) and shares a taste of the inexpressible experience he had of being "caught up to Paradise" (12:2–4), probably to counter such false claims made by those masquerad[ing] "as servants of righteousness" (11:15).

Paul on monetary giving

The other major topic of Second Corinthians is Paul's discussion of giving in chapters 8 and 9. Paul begins by alluding to the Macedonians, who first gave themselves to the Lord and to Paul (8:5), and who gave their money "in rich generosity" (8:2–3) in the midst of "the most severe trial" and "extreme poverty" (8:2).

There is also the example of Christ, who, "though he was rich, yet for your sakes he became poor" (8:9).

To be practical, giving should be according to a person's means (8:11), and God accepts it as such (8:12). The point is equality of means (8:13–14), a sharing of the resources God has put at our disposal.

Yet, having said that, Paul is anxious that the Corinthians not ignore
- the law of harvest—"Whoever sows generously will also reap generously" (9:6)
- the law of God's blessing—"God is able to make all grace abound to you, so that in all things at all times, having all that you need, you will abound in every good work" (9:8)
- the return blessing from the recipients—"Men will praise God for the obedience that accompanies your confession of the gospel of Christ, and for your generosity in sharing with them and with everyone else" (9:13–14)
- the example God gave us—"Thanks be to God for his indescribable gift!" (9:15)

Clash with the Judaizers

We alluded to the problem Paul faced by zealous Jewish believers who were insisting on Law-keeping. In the next chapter we look at Galatians, where this confrontation between Paul and the Judaizers becomes full-blown.

"Second mile" questions and topics

1. Paul calls the gospel of Christ crucified the "power of God and the wisdom of God" (1 Corinthians 1:24). Reflect on 1:18–31 and try to discover how these two words, *power* and *wisdom*, apply respectively to Jews and Greeks.

2. In First Corinthians 10:1–5 Paul alludes to the time when Israel was being guided from Egypt to the Promised Land. What are the "examples" Paul says we should take from these experiences (see 10:6–14)?

3. Memorize First Corinthians 13.

4. According to First Corinthians 15:3–5, what are the core elements of Paul's gospel preaching?

5. Second Corinthians 5:17 calls the one who is in Christ "a new creation." What, according to 5:14–15, is Paul's logic for such a statement? What should our being new creations motivate us to do? (See 5:18–20.)

The Urgent Letter
Galatians

Into the Word Each Day

1. Galatians 1:11–24 — Paul's testimony
2. Galatians 3:1–9 — Faith—not human effort
3. Galatians 3:26—4:7 — Sons of God
4. Galatians 5:1, 13–18 — Called to be free
5. Galatians 5:19–25 — The fruit of the Spirit
6. Galatians 6:1–5 — Bearing others' burdens
7. Galatians 6:14–18 — Boasting in the cross

AFTER OUR QUITE HURRIED LOOK at First and Second Corinthians, it will be well to pause briefly again before we consider the relatively short letter to the Galatians.

The New Testament is composed of "books." Some of them are historical in format, such as the four Gospels and especially Acts. Some are open letters to churches, such as Romans and First and Second Corinthians. A few are personal letters. The concluding book foretells future events. All were written under the inspiration of God's Holy Spirit (see 2 Timothy 3:16 and compare it with 2 Peter 3:16) so that what we have is an accurate, authoritative Word from God.

But intertwined with the message of these books are people —scores of them. Some appear briefly and not again. Others become familiar figures as we read the New Testament. The central Person of the Gospels and, indeed, of all the New Testament is Jesus Christ. A few of Jesus' disciples, particularly Peter, James, John, figure prominently. Then there are Jesus' cousin, John the Baptist, who prepared the way for Jesus and His public ministry; Nicodemus, the Jewish Pharisee who had a nighttime interview with Jesus; Pilate, the Roman governor who almost let Jesus go free, but who bowed to pressure and had Him crucified; Stephen, the godly man who became the first Christian martyr; Philip the evangelist, who baptized the treasurer of Ethiopia; Lydia, the business woman who helped found the church at Philippi. These are just a few of the dozens of interesting people we meet in the New Testament.

Paul, apostle to the Gentiles

Standing head-and-shoulders above all but Jesus Himself is Paul, originally Saul, the persecutor turned proponent, in many ways the greatest missionary ever to obey Jesus' command to "go and make disciples of all nations" (Matthew 28:19).

The first mention of Saul in Acts 7:57 is a hint of his intense character: as the Jews prepared to stone Stephen to death, "the witnesses laid their clothes at the feet of a young man named Saul." Acts 8:1 reads, "And Saul was there [as Stephen was stoned], giving approval to his death."

Stephen's death may have been the catalyst that stirred Saul to begin "to destroy the church" (8:3). Systematically, thoroughly, he set about on his personal agenda: "Going from house to house, he dragged off men and women and put them in prison" (8:3).

But God had mercy on Saul—as Saul later says, "because I acted in ignorance and unbelief" (1 Timothy 1:13). And God had His own agenda for the young persecutor: " 'This man is my chosen instrument to carry my name before the Gentiles and their kings and before the people of Israel' " (Acts 9:15). On a trip to Damascus to ferret out Christians, "suddenly a light from heaven flashed around him" (Acts 9:3). "He fell to the ground and heard a voice say to him, 'Saul, Saul, why do you persecute me?' " (9:4). Few conversions have been as dramatic. "At once he began to preach in the synagogues that Jesus is the Son of God" (9:20).

As Saul/Paul will tell us in Galatians, the comments of Christians in Judea were these: " 'The man who formerly persecuted us is now preaching the faith he once tried to destroy' " (Galatians 1:23). And Paul adds, "And they praised God because of me" (1:24).

Paul ponders the new revelation

It is from Paul's personal testimony in Galatians that we know he "went immediately into Arabia" (1:17) following his conversion and later returned to Damascus, the city where he had had the face-to-face encounter with Jesus. What did he do in Arabia? We can at least conjecture that he spent the time in seclusion, mentally reconciling his experience of conversion with all that he knew of the Old Testament Law and Jewish tradition—receiving "by revelation from Jesus Christ" (1:12) the message he thereafter preached.

Three years following his conversion, Paul "went up to Jerusalem to get acquainted with Peter and stayed with him fifteen days" (1:18). Besides Peter he saw only Jesus' brother James (1:19). He spent the next nine years in relative seclusion in Syria and Cilicia (Tarsus, capital of Cilicia, was Paul's birthplace—see Acts 9:11), until Barnabas recruited him to help the young church in Antioch (Acts 11:19–26).

Impending famine conditions (see Acts 11:27–28) prompted

the Antiochene Christians to send monetary help to "the brothers living in Judea," which they did "by Barnabas and Saul" (11:29–30). That seems to be the Jerusalem visit Paul refers to in Galatians 2:1. It gave him opportunity to meet "privately" with "those who seemed to be leaders" in order to verify that his understanding of the Christian way coincided with theirs (2:2–3).

Paul says, "Those men added nothing to my message. On the contrary, they saw that I had been given the task of preaching the gospel to the Gentiles, just as Peter had been given the task of preaching the gospel to the Jews" (2:6–7). James, Peter and John gave Paul "the right hand of fellowship," signifying accord with his message, and "agreed that we should go to the Gentiles, and they to the Jews" (2:9). By a year later, probably A.D. 47, Paul and Barnabas received their appointment to missionary service (see Acts 13:1–3).

Galatia

It was on their first mission that Paul and Barnabas founded the churches to which Paul's letter to the Galatians is addressed.

Galatia was the central region of Asia Minor, an area whose boundaries tended to change from time to time. In its more extensive eras it included Pisidia and Lycaonia, and therefore the towns of Pisidian Antioch, Iconium, Lystra and Derbe, mentioned in Acts 13 and 14. The people of Galatia— the Romans called them *Galli*—were largely barbarians who had poured over the peninsula in the third century before Christ. They had little religion of their own and easily adopted the superstitions and mythology of the Greeks. Likely many Greeks remained in Galatia in Paul's time. Phrygians, another segment of the population, held a lower social position. There were also great numbers of Jews, an indication that the area was favorable to commerce and trade.

Paul revisited the area with Silas on his second mission, "strengthening the churches" (Acts 15:41). Sometime after that visit Judaizing teachers descended on the still-young churches, declaring that only Gentiles who were circumcised and who observed the Law of Moses could be saved, and attacking Paul's missionary work.

When Paul heard that these converts were departing from the fundamental gospel of salvation by faith in Christ alone that he had preached among them, he wrote to try to counteract the false teaching they were accepting. Galatians was penned probably in A.D. 53, perhaps from Antioch just before Paul set out on his third mission.

The letter is the severest in tone of all Paul's writings. Contrary to his usual custom, Paul begins it with no word of thanksgiving or commendation. Instead, he begins by expressing surprise that the Galatian believers have departed from the pure faith (Galatians 1:6). Twice he pronounces an emphatic curse on those who are turning them from the truth (1:8–9).

The letter is in three parts. Chapters 1 and 2 are personal. Paul relates his own testimony and defends his apostolic authority. Chapters 3 and 4 are didactic or doctrinal. Paul explains and illustrates the message of salvation by faith apart from Law. Chapters 5 and 6 are practical. Paul describes the resulting freedom that comes through salvation by faith in Christ.

The two personal chapters

A key verse for Galatians is 2:16: "A man is not justified by observing the law, but by faith in Jesus Christ." Salvation by faith alone is the emphasis that Paul makes time and again in this short letter.

As in Second Corinthians, Paul defends his apostleship. He does so because it was necessary to the validation of his message. Paul wants these Christians to know that the gospel he preached was "not something that man made up" (1:11).

The authority of his message rested on his authority as a bona fide apostle of Jesus Christ. He begins the letter by declaring his apostleship. He claims he was "sent . . . by Jesus Christ and God the Father" (1:1) and proceeds, as we have noted, to state that the message he had received by revelation had the approval of the other apostles.

In an interesting vignette Paul remembers how Peter had visited Antioch while Paul was ministering there to the largely Gentile church. Peter ate with the Gentiles until some other Christians from the Jerusalem church arrived. Then "he began to draw back and separate himself from the Gentiles because," Paul says, "he was afraid of those who belonged to the circumcision group" (2:12). This produced a domino effect until "even Barnabas was led astray" (2:13).

Feisty Paul took on the venerable Peter in verbal combat. " 'You are a Jew, yet you live like a Gentile and not like a Jew. How is it, then, that you force Gentiles to follow Jewish customs? . . . We . . . have put our faith in Christ Jesus that we may be justified by faith in Christ and not by observing the law, because by observing the law no one will be justified'" (2:14–16). Paul continues with a statement that has become a favorite quotation: " 'I have been crucified with Christ and I no longer live, but Christ lives in me. The life I live in the body, I live by faith in the Son of God, who loved me and gave himself for me'" (2:20). He concludes by declaring: " 'If righteousness could be gained through the law, Christ died for nothing!'" (2:21).

It would be interesting to know how Peter, never at a loss for words, answered Paul!

The doctrinal part

In chapters 3 and 4 Paul cites three analogies from the Old Testament to drive home his argument. Two of them involve Abraham, the highly revered patriarch of the Jewish nation, as we noted in our look at Romans. Abraham lived 500 years before the Law and therefore is an illustration of justification by faith apart from Law.

Abraham *believed* God, Paul points out, quoting Genesis 15:6: " 'He believed God, and it was credited to him as righteousness'" (3:6). The Law, by contrast, is based on works, and again Paul quotes from the Old Testament, this time from Leviticus 18:5: " 'The man who does these things will live by them'" (Galatians 3:12). Moreover, the Law is an exacting taskmaster, requiring absolute and perfect obedience: " 'Cursed is everyone who does not continue to do everything written in the Book of the Law'" (3:10, quoting Deuteronomy 27:26). Since no one is absolutely perfect, "no one is justified before God by the law" (3:11).

But when we were in that predicament, "Christ redeemed us from the curse of the law by becoming a curse for us, for it is written: 'Cursed is everyone who is hung on a tree'" (3:13, quoting Deuteronomy 23:23).

In chapter 4 Paul switches the analogy from Abraham to that of a minor child in a household. He may be the family heir, but as long as he is a minor "he is no different from a slave, although he owns the whole estate" (4:1). Until he has reached a predetermined age "he is subject to guardians and trustees" (4:2).

So also were the Galatian readers of Paul's letter: "We were in slavery under the basic principles of the world" (4:3). "But when the time had fully come, God sent his Son, born of a woman, born under law, to redeem those under law, that we might receive the full rights of sons" (4:4). Moreover, "God sent the Spirit of his Son into our hearts, the Spirit who calls out, '*Abba,* Father'" (4:6; cf. Romans 8:15–16). As a result, Paul declares, believers in Christ are sons, not slaves, and heirs (4:7).

The analogy of Abraham's two sons

In 4:22 Paul draws on still another Old Testament analogy: Abraham's two sons, Ishmael and Isaac. Abraham and his wife, Sarah, well along in years, were childless. This was both an embarrassment to Sarah and a concern to Abraham, who had no successor. In one of his talks with God, Abraham voiced his distress about this, and God promised him an heir and a posterity as uncountable as the stars of the heavens (see Genesis 15:2–5).

Years went by, and when there was no sign of God's promise, Sarah convinced Abraham that he should consider her maid, Hagar.

"'Go, sleep with my maidservant,'" Sarah said to Abraham; "'perhaps I can build a family through her'" (Genesis 16:2). And in due course Hagar bore Ishmael. Abraham at the time was 86 years old (Genesis 16:16). But Ishmael was not the son of promise.

When Abraham was 100, Sarah bore him Isaac—the son God had said He would send (21:2-5).

Paul sees in this familiar bit of history an analogy that fits the Galatian Christians, now tempted to turn back "to those weak and miserable principles" of Law-keeping (Galatians 4:9). Hagar and Sarah, the slave woman and the free, "represent two covenants," Paul says (4:24). Hagar represents the covenant of Law, symbolized by Mount Sinai, where the Law was given to Israel, and Jerusalem, where the covenant of Law is perpetuated. It is a regimen of slavery to a legal system (see 4:25). Sarah represents "the Jerusalem that is above" and the freedom it symbolizes.

Even as Ishmael mocked the younger Isaac to the point where Abraham had to send Ishmael and his mother away (Genesis 21:8–14), so the Judaizers are persecuting the free-born children of God (Galatians 4:28–29). The antidote now, as then: "'Get rid of the slave woman and her son'" (4:30).

The practical part

Paul begins the practical part of his letter by declaring, "It is for freedom that Christ has set us free" (5:1). Therefore he urges the Galatians to "stand firm" and not to let themselves "be burdened again by a yoke of slavery."

Second, he tells them to "live by the Spirit" so that they "will not gratify the desires of the sinful nature" (5:16). The inner conflict that Paul described in Romans 7 he mentions again here (5:17). "But if you are led by the Spirit," he adds, "you are not under law" (5:18).

In case there is any doubt as to what "the acts of the sinful nature" (5:19) are, Paul catalogs 15 of them (5:19–21). He follows that list with the fruit of the Spirit: "love, joy, peace, patience, kindness, goodness, faithfulness, gentleness and self-control" (5:22–23), adding, "Against such things there is no law."

He continues, "Those who belong to Christ Jesus have crucified the sinful nature with its passions and desires. Since we live by the Spirit, let us keep in step with the Spirit" (5:24–25).

But the ideal is frequently above the actual. Walking in the Spirit and bearing the fruit of the Spirit are the objectives, but sometimes we fall short. "Brothers," Paul exhorts, "if someone is caught in a sin, you who are spiritual should restore him gently. But watch yourself, or you also may be tempted" (6:1).

We are to "carry each other's burdens," and in this way "fulfill the law of Christ" (6:2). Each of us is to "test his own actions" (6:4). The apparent discrepancy between the exhortation in 6:2 to carry one another's burdens and the observation in 6:5 that "each one should carry his own load" is clearer in the original Greek language from which our translation was made. "Burden" refers to a weight or load that exceeds the strength of the one carrying it. It could be a sorrow, a personal problem or financial distress. "Load" refers here to responsibility, the point being that we are not to compare ourselves with others (6:4) but "test [our] own actions" and stand responsible before God for them.

Paul even has a word concerning the remuneration of teachers: "Anyone who receives instruction in the word must share all good things with his instructor" (6:6).

His summation: "A man reaps what he sows. The one who sows to please his sinful nature, from that nature will reap destruction; the one who sows to please the Spirit, from the Spirit will reap eternal life. Let us not become weary in doing good, for at the proper time we will reap a harvest if we do not give up" (6:7–9).

In his brief conclusion, beginning with 6:11, Paul talks about the "large letters" with which he wrote. Paul seems to have been suffering from a disease of the eyes that made it difficult or impossible for him to see fine print. He says in 4:15, "You would have torn out your eyes and given them to me"—an indication that the problem was already evident at the time of his visit to the Galatian churches.

The verse also implies that Paul penned this letter himself, rather than relying on one of his traveling companions to write as he dictated—possibly an indication that Paul was alone at the time but felt the message was too urgent to await a scribe.

Even in the conclusion, Paul makes one more attempt to underscore his important word to the churches: "Those who want to make a good impression outwardly are trying to compel you to be circumcised. The only reason they do this is to avoid being persecuted for the cross of Christ. Not even those who are circumcised obey the law, yet they want you to be circumcised that they may boast about your flesh. May I never boast except in the cross of our Lord Jesus Christ, through which the world has been crucified to me, and I to the world" (6:12–14).

Although Paul begins with no commendation of the Galatians, he closes with a benediction: "The grace of our Lord Jesus Christ be with your spirit, brothers. Amen" (6:18).

A look ahead

With the conclusion of Galatians we have completed our look at the four letters of Paul that—from our vantage point— deal particularly with personal salvation through Christ. This salvation is the theme of Romans, as we noted. It is a definite element permeating First and Second Corinthians. As we have seen in this chapter, it is the theme of Galatians. Sometimes these four books are termed *soteriological*—from the Greek word for salvation.

We come next to three letters Paul wrote while he was under house arrest in Rome: Ephesians, Philippians, Colossians. Along with the short letter to Philemon, they are frequently called the prison epistles. Their central theme is Jesus Christ, so they are sometimes described as *Christological* in content.

Ephesians, Philippians and Colossians are followed by two letters to the church in Thessalonica—First and Second Thessalonians. The theme of those letters is Christ's pending return and the circumstances surrounding that end-time event. Another Greek word has been borrowed to describe the second-coming emphasis of First and Second Thessalonians —*eschatological*.

After the two eschatological books, we have First and Second Timothy and Titus, three letters written to young men in the ministry. Because those three letters are particularly concerned about church matters, they are described by the Greek word for church—*ecclesiological*.

Philemon, Paul's short personal letter to the man of that name, follows immediately after Titus, so we will consider it along with the three ecclesiological letters, even though its theme falls more appropriately with the three Christological letters.

The next chapter, then, will look at the prison letters. Prepare yourself for some of Paul's most spiritually exalted writing!

"Second mile" questions and topics

1. Memorize the two verses that center so firmly on the cross of Jesus Christ: Galatians 2:20 and Galatians 6:14. What similarities do you find between these two verses and Second Corinthians 5:14–15?

2. Compare Galatians 6:1–2 and Paul's concern that the erring Christian be restored, with Jesus' words in Matthew 18:15–17. What do these two passages say about Christ's love for His Church? How can we be partners with Him in His loving concern?

7

Three Letters from Rome
Ephesians, Philippians, Colossians

Into the Word Each Day

1. Ephesians 1:15–23   To know Jesus better
2. Ephesians 6:10–18   The whole armor
3. Philippians 1:3–11   More and more love
4. Philippians 2:5–11   Jesus' example
5. Philippians 3:4b–11   "I want to know Christ"
6. Colossians 1:9–20   The supreme Jesus
7. Colossians 3:1–10   Rules for resurrected people

IN CHAPTER 6 WE TOOK A long look at Paul the apostle and his career from the days when he was a dedicated persecutor of the church to the years of his dedicated church-planting work.

In the course of three missionary journeys, Paul and his several coworkers established churches throughout much of Asia Minor and Greece. In the process they set the course of Christian penetration westward through Europe rather than eastward toward the Orient.

Back in Jerusalem, in the temple, where Paul had gone to fulfill a rite urged on him by James and the elders (Acts 21:24), some Asian Jews spied him and stirred the multitude (21:27). Caesar's forces stepped in to preserve Paul from the angry mob (21:33–34). His incarceration there in Jerusalem began an imprisonment that was to last nearly five years and possibly longer—two of them in Caesarea (24:27) and two of them in Rome under house arrest (28:30).

It was during Paul's imprisonment in Rome (A.D. 60–62) that he did some of his greatest work, for at least four of his letters originated during that imprisonment. Three of the four—Ephesians, Philippians and Colossians—are considered to be some of the most sublime writing anywhere in the Scriptures. Since we want to look at all three in this one chapter, we will turn immediately to them.

There are similarities

Surveying three such important books in such a brief space would be less possible were it not that the three bear similarities. Especially is this true of Ephesians and Colossians. We have already mentioned that all three are Christological in character, focusing on the person of Jesus Christ.

All three begin with a brief salutation, a note of praise, a prayer. All three stress the practical need to live worthy of the Christian calling.

In Ephesians Paul prays that Christ may indwell the hearts of his readers. To the Colossians he speaks of "Christ in you, the hope of glory" (1:27). In both Ephesians and Philippians Paul urges Christian maturity.

Two of them bear special exhortation to wives and husbands, to children and parents, to slaves and masters (Ephesians 5:22—6:9, Colossians 3:18—4:1). Paul asks both groups of readers to pray for him and his ministry (Ephesians 6:19–20; Colossians 4:2–3).

To whom the letters were addressed

Ephesus, located on the western coast of Asia Minor, was the chief city of Asia Minor. It was a center of idolatry. The temple of Artemis (Diana—King James Version) was one of the seven ancient wonders of the world. A hillside amphitheater could seat 25,000.

Paul's first visit to Ephesus was a brief one at the end of his second mission (Acts 18:18–19). In the course of his third mission (Acts 19:1 ff.) he ministered there two or three years, firmly establishing the Christian church not only in Ephesus but in the surrounding regions (19:10).

Although Paul's letter "to the Ephesians" bears that name, there is some probability that it originally was a circular letter intended for all the churches of the area. The two oldest manuscripts do not contain the words "in Ephesus" in 1:1, the letter contains no greetings to specific individuals, and a reference in Colossians 4:16 to "the letter from Laodicea" points possibly to the letter we know as Ephesians.

Colossae was little more than a country town a hundred miles east of Ephesus in the Lycus Valley of Asia Minor, an area noted for religious syncretism. It is probable that the church in Colossae was brought to birth by Epaphras during Paul's years at Ephesus (see Colossians 1:7–8).

Philippi, a major city of Macedonia that carried colony status in the Roman Empire, was the first city in what we know today as Europe to receive the gospel. Paul was divinely led westward to Philippi. After being hindered from preaching further in Asia Minor, Paul saw a vision of a Macedonian man calling, " 'Come over to Macedonia and help us' " (Acts 16:9). Paul's initial experiences at Philippi are related in the rest of Acts 16. Twice more, during his third mission, Paul visited Philippi and the largely Gentile Philippian church (Acts 20:1–6).

Ephesians

Ephesians falls into a natural two-part division, chapters 1–3 being doctrinal and chapters 4–6 practical. The church, the body of Christ, is the overall theme—a church that has been blessed "with every spiritual blessing in Christ" (1:3).

Paul begins with the spiritual blessings his Christian readers have. God "chose" them "before the creation" for the purpose of making them "holy and blameless in his sight" (1:4), and "for the praise of his glory" (1:12). To accomplish this, He "predestined" their "adoption as his sons" (1:5), redeemed them "through Christ's blood" (1:7), and sealed them with "the promised Holy Spirit" (1:13). God's purpose in all of this was to "bring all things in heaven and on earth together under one head, even Christ" (1:10).

The staggering impact of God's great design launches Paul into a rhapsody of thanksgiving and a prayer. "I keep asking," he says, "that . . . God . . . may give you the Spirit of wisdom and revelation, so that you may know him better (1:15–18). He wants them to know

- "the hope to which [God] has called you" (1:18)
- "the riches of his glorious inheritance in the saints" (1:18)
- "his incomparably great power for us who believe" (1:19)— a power demonstrated when God raised Christ "from the dead and seated him at his right hand in the heavenly realms, far above" every other kind of rule and authority in this age or the next (1:20–21) and made Him "head over everything for the church, which is his body, the fullness of him who fills everything in every way" (1:22–23)

Made alive in Christ

His readers had once been dead in their "transgressions and sins" (2:1). Paul includes himself and says we gratified "the cravings of our sinful nature and followed its desires and thoughts" (2:3). "But because of his great love for us, God . . . made us alive with Christ" (2:4–5). He "raised us up with Christ and seated us with him in the heavenly realms" (2:6) "that in the coming ages he might show the incomparable riches of his grace, expressed in his kindness to us in Christ Jesus" (2:7). (Are you beginning to catch the sublime language and exalted concepts of this book?)

The aliveness with Christ (2:5) was designed to accomplish another purpose: God wanted to obliterate the age-old distinction between Jew and Gentile. "Formerly you who are Gentiles . . . were . . . excluded from citizenship in Israel and foreigners to the covenants of the promise," Paul says. "But now in Christ Jesus you who once were far away have been brought near through the blood of Christ" (2:11–13).

"Consequently," Paul continues, "you are . . . fellow citizens with God's people" (2:19). "You too are being built together to become a dwelling in which God lives by his Spirit" (2:22).

Paul digresses at the beginning of chapter 3 to talk about his apostleship to the Gentiles, a subject he covered in some depth in the letter to the Galatians and in the Corinthian correspondence. He ends the first half of the letter with a sublime prayer that his readers "may be filled to the measure of all the fullness of God" (3:19).

Building up the Body of Christ

Having completed the doctrinal part of the letter, Paul moves on to its practical application. "Live a life worthy of the calling you have received," he urges his readers (4:1). They should "be completely humble and gentle" (4:2) and "patient, bearing with one another in love" (4:2).

To the church God has given gifts: "some to be apostles,

some to be prophets, some to be evangelists, and some to be pastors and teachers" (4:11). The purpose of these gifts is "to prepare God's people for works of service so that the body of Christ may be built up until we all reach unity in the faith and in the knowledge of the Son of God and become mature, attaining to the whole measure of the fullness of Christ" (4:12–13). Paul employs the analogy of the human body to demonstrate how this works (4:14–16).

Living as children of light

Although most of his readers are Gentiles, Paul insists that they "no longer live as the Gentiles do" in "every kind of impurity" (4:17, 19). Rather he says, "Put off your old self, . . . be made new in the attitude of your minds; and . . . put on the new self, created to be like God in true righteousness and holiness" (4:22–24).

He goes on to list ten prohibitions (4:25—5:4) and a dozen positive admonitions (4:25—5:20).

Paul focuses on three interpersonal relationships: wives and husbands, children and parents, slaves and masters. The first two still apply directly; the third by extension may apply to the employer-employee relationship more common today. Wives are to submit (5:22); husbands are to love (5:25). Children are to obey (6:1), fathers are not to "exasperate" them but "instead, bring them up in the training and instruction of the Lord" (6:4). Slaves are to obey (6:5); masters are not to threaten (6:9).

The armor of God

Paul sees the Christian life as a warfare—a "struggle . . . against the rulers, against the authorities, against the powers of this dark world and against the spiritual forces of evil in the heavenly realms" (6:12). Therefore we need "the full armor of God" (6:11) which includes

the belt of truth
the breastplate of righteousness
"feet fitted with the readiness that comes from the gospel
    of peace"
the shield of faith
the helmet of salvation
the sword of the Spirit (the Word of God) (6:14-17)

We are to "pray in the Spirit" (6:18), and Paul asks that his readers pray for him, too.

He concludes his letter with a brief commendation of Tychicus, bearer of the missive, and a benediction.

Philippians

Philippians is the letter of joy. No congregation held a deeper place in Paul's affections. His letter is full of praise and thanksgiving. The word "joy" or its derivatives occur 14 times in the four chapters. It is difficult to imagine that Paul was in bonds (1:13) when he wrote.

No systematic outline is possible. Paul alternates between instruction and personal references just as anyone writing a letter to dear friends might do.

The letter was prompted by financial assistance the church had conveyed through Epaphroditus (4:10–18), and the assistance seems to have reached Paul in a time of great need. Not only their gifts but the concern represented by the gifts cheered the apostle greatly.

So it is appropriate that Paul should begin the letter by a statement of praise: "I thank my God every time I remember you" (1:3). He looks on the Philippians as partners in the gospel (1:7), and prays that their "love may abound more and more in knowledge and depth of insight" (1:9).

Paul is glad to report that imprisonment has not meant a cessation of gospel witness. "It has become clear throughout the whole palace guard and to everyone else that I am in chains for Christ," he says (1:13). This, in turn, has emboldened other believers "to speak the word of God more courageously and fearlessly" (1:14). Near the end of his letter he conveys the greeting of "all the saints, . . . especially those who belong in Caesar's household" (4:22). We can only wonder if there were Christians in Caesar's household *before* Paul's Roman imprisonment.

Paul has to admit that not all who "preach Christ" do so from a right motive (1:15–17), but "the important thing is that . . . Christ is preached" (1:18)—and for that Paul rejoices.

In the uncertainty and even hardship of his status as a prisoner, Paul weighs the decided advantages of being "with Christ" (1:23), that is, in His heavenly presence, but he concludes that "it is more necessary for you [Philippians] that I remain in the body" and believes that such will be the case (1:25).

Unity in Philippi

As with the readers of his Ephesians letter, Paul is concerned for unity in the Philippian church. Reported contentions between coworkers of Paul, Euodia and Syntyche (4:2), are probably what trigger his exhortation to be "one in spirit and purpose" (2:2)—which, in turn, prompts Paul's recital of one of the great and probably one of the earliest Christological statements: Philippians 2:5–11. Paul declares that Christ Jesus, "being in very nature God" (2:6), "made himself nothing, taking the very nature of a servant" (2:7) and became "obedient to death—even death on a cross!" (2:8).

Because Jesus was so willingly obedient,

<blockquote>

God exalted him to the highest place
and gave him the name that is above every name,
that at the name of Jesus every knee should bow,
in heaven and on earth and under the earth,
and every tongue confess that Jesus Christ is Lord,
to the glory of God the Father

Philippians 2:9–11.

</blockquote>

Paul's applications: Have the same attitude Jesus had (2:5), and "do everything without complaining or arguing" (2:14).

Paul once more cites his pedigree as a circumcised "Hebrew of Hebrews" (3:4; 2 Corinthians 11:22). But he says, "I will consider everything a loss compared to the surpassing greatness of knowing Christ Jesus my Lord, for whose sake I have lost all things" (3:8). He continues, "I want to know Christ and the power of his resurrection and the fellowship of sharing in his sufferings, becoming like him in his death, and so, somehow, to attain to the resurrection from the dead" (3:10–11). So, "forgetting what is behind and straining toward what is ahead, I press on toward the goal to win the prize for which God has called me heavenward in Christ Jesus" (3:13–14).

Four other frequently quoted verses appear in chapter 4:

- "Do not be anxious about anything, but in everything, by prayer and petition, with thanksgiving, present your requests to God" (4:6)
- "Whatever is true, whatever is noble, whatever is right, whatever is pure, whatever is lovely, whatever is admirable—if anything is excellent or praiseworthy—think about such things" (4:8)
- "I can do everything through him who gives me strength" (4:13)
- "My God will meet all your needs according to his glorious riches in Christ Jesus" (4:19)

Colossians

We have already mentioned some of the similarities that made Colossians and Ephesians "twin" letters. In Ephesians Paul concentrates on the nature of the church. In Colossians he concentrates on the exalted position of Christ, the Head of the church.

As we noted earlier, Colossae was a small, rural town, and probably the church was not large. Why, of the many churches in the area, did it rate a special letter from Paul? The answer can be conjectured from the fact that Epaphras, the probable founder of the Colossian church (1:7), had visited Paul in Rome (4:12, 13) conveying to him the material gift of the Philippians, and no doubt advising him at the same time of an incipient heresy that had cropped up in the small church at Colossae.

This heresy arose from the age-old problem of good and evil. How could a good and holy God create a world obviously evil and sinful? There began to grow a popular current of thought eventually called Gnosticism (from the Greek word for knowledge). Gnosticism explained the anomaly by removing God from the actual creation process. Imagine for a moment the ripple effect created when a stone is dropped into a pool. That first ripple, out there in the center, the gnostics said, is symbolic of God in holy aloofness. The rings emanating from the center illustrate a succession of angels, each more distant from God the Source, each a little less holy. Finally you come to the Old Testament Jehovah, who was sufficiently unholy that He could create a sinful world. Somewhere among the "ripples" of angels was a Christ who really had not become enfleshed (since gnostics looked upon flesh as inherently sinful).

The gnostics were guilty of at least four theological errors: (1) Christ only *appeared* to be in human form, (2) Jehovah of the Old Testament was sinful and thus inferior to the true God, whom they termed the Fullness or the All, (3) the body being evil, was deserving of punishment and denial, (4) there would be no resurrection of the body. In addition they held unbiblical theories about angels.

The supremacy of Christ

Paul fires some broadsides at the gnostic error. His references to Jesus include the following:
- "the image [the perfect manifestation] of the invisible God, the firstborn over all creation" (1:15) and declares that "by him all things were created" (1:16)
- the One "before all things," the One "in [whom] all things hold together" (1:17)
- "the head of the body, the church" (1:18)
- "the firstborn from among the dead, so that in everything he might have the supremacy" (1:18)

Paul says that in Jesus "God was pleased to have all his fullness dwell" (1:19). The term "fullness," as we have noted, was one the gnostics used when they referred to the Source or the All.

In quick strokes Paul cuts away all the postulates of the gnostics and leaves standing in transcendent splendor a peerless Jesus, very God of very God, who has made "peace through his blood, shed on the cross" (1:20).

Paul says, "I have become [the church's] servant by the commission God gave me to present to you the word of God in its fullness—the mystery . . . now disclosed to the saints" (1:25–26), namely, "Christ in you, the hope of glory" (1:27).

He declares that in Christ "are hidden all the treasures of wisdom and knowledge" (2:3), and adds: "I tell you this so that no one may deceive you by fine-sounding arguments" (2:4).

Freedom from human regulations

Paul still has the gnostic heresy in view when he says

- "So then, just as you received Christ Jesus as Lord, continue to live in him, rooted and built up in him, strengthened in the faith as you were taught, and overflowing with thankfulness" (2:6)
- "See to it that no one takes you captive through hollow and deceptive philosophy" (2:8)
- "In Christ all the fullness of the Deity lives in bodily form, and you have been given fullness in Christ, who is the head over every power and authority" (2:9–10)
- "Therefore do not let anyone judge you by what you eat or drink, or with regard to a religious festival, a New Moon celebration or a Sabbath day" (2:16)
- "Do not let anyone who delights in false humility and the worship of angels disqualify you for the prize" (2:18)

As in his letter to the Philippians, Paul sounds a positive note to govern human behavior: "Since, then, you have been raised with Christ, set your hearts on things above, where Christ is seated at the right hand of God. Set your minds on things above, not on earthly things. For you died, and your life is now hidden with Christ in God. . . . Put to death, therefore, whatever belongs to your earthly nature" (3:1–5).

With richness of expression Paul exhorts the Colossians to "clothe [themselves] with compassion," to "bear with each other," to "forgive . . . grievances," to "put on love," to let the "peace of Christ" rule in their hearts, to "be thankful," to "let the word of Christ dwell in [them] richly," to "do . . . all in the name of the Lord Jesus, giving thanks to God the Father through him" (3:12–17).

The letter closes with some further instructions and final greetings.

"Second mile" questions and topics

1. In Ephesians 6:11–18, Paul likens the Christian life to earthly warfare and the Christian to a Roman soldier. Which pieces of equipment are especially for defense? Which are especially for offensive use? What provision, if any, is made in case of retreat?

2. Philippians 2:7 says Jesus "made himself nothing [literally, emptied himself]." What were the successive steps in His self-emptying?

3. In Colossians 2:20—3:4, Paul contrasts legalistic living by regulations with living "above, where Christ is." In your own words, describe these two attitudes and their implications for behavior.

8

Jesus Will Return
First and Second Thessalonians

Into the Word Each Day

JESUS' EVENTUAL RETURN TO EARTH is a persistent theme running through the New Testament. His return often is referred to as the Second Advent or Second Coming, to distinguish it from His first appearance as Mary's Baby.

Jesus Himself spoke at considerable length to His disciples about His Second Advent. Matthew gives us the fullest account of Jesus' message (Matthew 24—25). Because it was spoken while Jesus and His disciples were on the Mount of Olives (24:3), it frequently is called the Olivet Discourse.

What Jesus says about His return

Jesus' teachings on that occasion were triggered by an innocent exclamation by His disciples about the grandeur of the temple buildings (see Mark 13:1, where the same episode is reported). "'Do you see all these things?'" Jesus replied. "'I tell you the truth, not one stone here will be left on another; every one will be thrown down'" (Matthew 24:2).

Jesus' statement was so unexpected and so improbable (in human terms) that His followers immediately associated it with the end of the world. "'Tell us,' they said, 'when will this happen, and what will be the sign of your coming and of the end of the age?'" (Matthew 24:3). So Jesus proceeded to tell them.

He painted a troubled picture: deception by false christs (24:4–5), wars and rumors of wars (24:6), famines and earthquakes (24:7), persecution (24:9), a turning away from the faith and betrayal (24:10), false prophets (24:11), an increase of wickedness (24:12).

These developments will have an adverse effect on Christians. Jesus said, "'Many will turn away from the faith and will betray and hate each other'" (24:10). He said, "'The love of most will grow cold'" (24:12), "'but he who stands firm to the end will be saved'" (24:13). Then Jesus made a very significant statement: "'This gospel of the kingdom will be preached in the whole world as a testimony to all nations, and then the end will come'" (24:14). His words seem to be a reference to the worldwide proclamation of the gospel through missionary activity just prior to the end of the age. That kind of worldwide proclamation is now a reality through the efforts of missionaries from all parts of the world to all parts of the world and through radio and television.

The passage that follows tends to be confusing because of what happened historically in A.D. 70 when Roman forces led by Titus destroyed Jerusalem, literally leaving no temple stone atop another. Christians aware of Jesus' Olivet Discourse took Jesus' advice (24:16–18), fled the city and escaped with their lives. Possibly a half million other people died in the

Roman holocaust that effectively wiped out Israel as a nation.

Jesus, however, could not have been referring only to the tribulation of those days in A.D. 70, because He went on to say, "'Immediately after the distress of those days . . . they will see the Son of Man coming on the clouds of the sky, with power and great glory. And he will send his angels with a loud trumpet call, and they will gather his elect from the four winds, from one end of the heavens to the other'" (24:29–31). That did not happen following the A.D. 70 tribulation.

This leads us to believe, as other Scriptures indicate, that the Jews, having returned to their land, will reconstruct the temple in Jerusalem and again witness a similar desecration of it by outside forces. Many believe that the founding of Israel in 1948 and its subsequent national development is the prelude to these events Jesus referred to in His Olivet Discourse.

To His followers Jesus said, "'Keep watch, because you do not know on what day your Lord will come. . . . You must be ready, because the Son of Man will come at an hour when you do not expect him'" (24:42–44).

Other statements about Jesus' return

We have not only Jesus' own words regarding His return to earth, but at the time of His ascension to heaven (Acts 1:9–11), "two men dressed in white" promised the watching disciples: "'This same Jesus, who has been taken from you into heaven, will come back in the same way you have seen him go into heaven.'"

The return of Christ and the events leading up to it, His millennial reign on earth and the ultimate new heavens and new earth are the theme of most of Revelation, as we will later see.

This eschatological (end times) theme also receives frequent mention by Paul in his letters (e.g., Romans 16:19–20).

But especially it permeates both First and Second Thessalonians, the two letters we are looking at in this chapter. They are, as we mentioned before, the two earliest of Paul's preserved letters and possibly the earliest of any of the New Testament Scriptures.

Thessalonica

Thessalonica, present-day Salonika, was a large mercantile city located on the east-west highway through the province of Macedonia. A seaport with an excellent harbor, Thessalonica was the capital of the province.

The city had a sizeable Jewish population and a synagogue, which Paul and Silas used, "as his custom was" (Acts 17:2), to gain a foothold for the gospel. Although it would seem from the account in Acts 17:1–9 that Paul was in Thessalonica only a very short time, the stay was probably four or five months. Paul reminds the Philippians (Philippians 4:15–16) that they twice sent him aid while he was in Thessalonica, and this of itself would indicate at least some lapse of time.

A riot stirred up by Thessalonian Jews forced the departure of Paul and Silas, who then went to Berea (Acts 17:10). Paul continued on to Athens (17:14–15) and eventually to Corinth (18:1).

When Silas and Timothy rejoined Paul in Corinth, they brought him reports of the church in Thessalonica (Thessalonians 3:2–5). Although the young Christians had been faithful despite continued persecution, they were inwardly troubled by misunderstandings concerning the return of the Lord. Believing the return to be soon, some of them had stopped working and were living in idleness. Others were disturbed, not knowing the fate of fellow Christians who had died before the return of the Lord.

Paul's first letter to the Thessalonians was written to meet this situation. It is in two parts: the first a personal reference to his ministry among the Thessalonians (chapters 1—3), and the second, practical and doctrinal (chapters 4—5). Each division closes with a prayer. Although the chapter divisions were made many centuries later and are not a part of the original letter, each chapter happens to end with a reference to the Second Coming of Christ.

Paul's ministry in Thessalonica

Following a salutation that we have already observed is typical of Paul's letters, the apostle thanks God for the Thessalonian believers. He says, "We continually remember before our God and Father your work produced by faith, your labor prompted by love, and your endurance inspired by hope in our Lord Jesus Christ" (1:3).

"Our gospel," he continues, "came to you not simply with words, but also with power, with the Holy Spirit and with deep conviction" (1:5). They imitated Paul and in turn were "a model to all the believers in Macedonia and Achaia" (1:7). They "turned to God from idols to serve the living and true God, and to wait for his Son from heaven, whom he raised from the dead—Jesus, who rescues us from the coming wrath" (1:9–10).

In chapter 2 Paul reminds them of his entry into Thessalonica following his expulsion from Philippi, and how, "in spite of strong opposition," he "dared" to preach the gospel to them (2:2). The preaching was not just in word: "We loved you so much that we were delighted to share with you not only the gospel of God but our lives as well" (2:8). He and his team members "worked night and day in order not to be a burden to anyone" (2:9). They dealt with the Thessalonians "as a father deals with his own children, encouraging, comforting and urging [them] to live lives worthy of God" (2:11–12).

Paul confesses his "intense longing" (2:17) for the Thessalonians. "You are our glory and joy," he says (2:20). Not able to go himself, he "sent Timothy" (3:2) not merely to obtain news (3:5) but "to strengthen and encourage [them] in [their] faith" (3:2). The news Timothy brought back was most encouraging to Paul. "Now we really live," he says to them, "since you are standing firm in the Lord" (3:8).

Note Paul's prayer for the Thessalonians in 3:11–13: "Now may our God and Father himself and our Lord Jesus clear the way for us to come to you. May the Lord make your love increase and overflow for each other and for everyone else, just as ours does for you. May he strengthen your hearts so that you will be blameless and holy in the presence of our God and Father when our Lord Jesus comes with all his holy ones."

Living to please God

Paul begins the more admonitory part of his letter with practical admonitions. God wills that the Thessalonians should be holy (4:3), and this means no sexual immorality but rather bodily discipline (4:4–5). "God did not call us to be impure, but to live a holy life" (4:7).

To those who had given up work in anticipation of Jesus' near return, he says, "Work with your hands . . . so that your daily life may win the respect of outsiders and so that you will not be dependent on anybody" (4:11–12).

And that brings the apostle to the matter of the Lord's return and the question of the Thessalonian Christians about believers who had died prior to His coming. "We do not want you to be ignorant about those who fall asleep," he says (4:13). "We believe that Jesus died and rose again and so we believe that God will bring with Jesus those who have fallen asleep in him" (4:14). And then he launches into a statement that will quicken the heartbeat until the moment it is reality:

"According to the Lord's own word, . . . we who are still alive, who are left till the coming of the Lord, will certainly not precede those who have fallen asleep. For the Lord himself will come down from heaven, with a loud command, with the voice of the archangel and with the trumpet call of God, and the dead in Christ will rise first. After that, we who are still alive and are left will be caught up with them in the clouds to meet the Lord in the air. And so we will be with the Lord forever" (4:15–17).

Christians have come to put a technical term to this event. They call it the *rapture*, from a word meaning to be lifted up and carried away. Note that it involves all believers: first the dead in Christ, then we who are still alive. It is a very visible, public event. The Lord Himself descends "with a loud command, with the voice of the archangel and with the trumpet call of God." Note that it ushers in our permanent union with Jesus Christ: "So we will be with the Lord forever."

When?

The Thessalonians wanted to know when this would take place. We will see from Paul's second letter to them that some felt Paul had taught that the rapture had already taken place (2 Thessalonians 2:2).

"About times and dates we do not need to write to you," Paul says (1 Thessalonians 5:1). The day will come like a thief in the night. It will occur at a time when the general populace least expects it.

But believers "are not in darkness that this day should surprise" them (5:4). As "sons of the light and sons of the day" the Thessalonians should be "alert and self-controlled" (5:5–6). "God did not appoint us to suffer wrath," Paul says encouragingly, "but to receive salvation through our Lord Jesus Christ" (5:9).

Final instructions

Like a solicitous father, Paul dispenses final words of in-
struction before he signs off:
"Respect those . . . who are over you in the Lord" (5:2)
"Live in peace with each other" (5:13)
"Warn those who are idle" (5:14)
"Encourage the timid, help the weak" (5:14)
"Be patient with everyone" (5:14)
"Make sure that nobody pays back wrong for wrong" (5:15)
"Always try to be kind to each other and to everyone else"
    (5:15)
"Be joyful always" (5:16)
"Pray continually" (5:17)
"Give thanks in all circumstances" (5:18)
"Do not put out the Spirit's fire" (5:19)
"Do not treat prophecies with contempt" (5:20)
"Test everything. Hold on to the good. Avoid every kind
    of evil" (5:21–22)

Even Paul's final prayer emphasizes the Second Coming:
"May God himself, the God of peace, sanctify you through
and through. May your whole spirit, soul and body be kept
blameless at the coming of our Lord Jesus Christ. The one
who calls you is faithful and he will do it" (5:23–24).

Second Thessalonians

It is probable that Second Thessalonians was written very
shortly after First Thessalonians. The first letter had satisfied
their concern regarding believers who had died before Christ's
return, but the whole subject of the Second Coming was at
the surface of their thinking. Moreover, someone evidently
claimed that the Lord had returned already, attributing this
statement to the apostle Paul himself (see 2 Thessalonians

2:2). So part of Paul's purpose in his follow-up letter was to set the record straight and then to explain more fully the events that must transpire before Jesus returns.

Looking at this letter from the perspective of non-first-century Thessalonians, we are at a tantalizing disadvantage, for Paul refers cryptically to truth he taught the Thessalonians while he was with them (see 2:5–7). We can only guess to what he was referring.

It is evident from chapter 1 that the persecution of the believers at Thessalonica—something they had lived with almost from the very first (1 Thessalonians 1:6)—had not abated. Paul "boasts about [their] perseverance and faith in all the persecutions and trials [they] are enduring" (2 Thessalonians 1:4). But a day of recompense is coming: God will "pay back trouble to those who trouble [the Thessalonians] and give relief to [the ones] who are troubled" (1:6–7).

This will happen, Paul says, "when the Lord is revealed from heaven in blazing fire with his powerful angels. He will punish those who do not know God and do not obey the gospel of our Lord Jesus. They will be punished with everlasting destruction and shut out from the presence of the Lord and from the majesty of his power on the day he comes to be glorified in his holy people and to be marveled at among all those who have believed" (1:7–10).

The "man of lawlessness" must first appear

Regarding the statement, purportedly from Paul, that Jesus had returned already, the apostle denies the rumor and reminds them that certain events stand between them and the return of Christ. "That day will not come," he says, "until the rebellion occurs and the man of lawlessness is revealed, the man doomed to destruction" (2:3). Paul further describes this man of lawlessness as one who "opposes and exalts himself over everything that is called God or is worshiped, and even sets himself up in God's temple, proclaiming himself to be God" (2:4).

Something was "holding him back," delaying until "the proper time" his revelation (2:6). Paul saw no need to name either the "man" or this thing holding him back, inasmuch as Paul had made it clear to the Thessalonians while he was still with them. But that does not help us know to whom or what he referred. Paul says "the secret power of lawlessness is already at work," but that the one now holding it back "will continue to do so till he is taken out of the way" (2:7).

When that happens, the lawless one will have utter freedom in the world. His satanic power will be evidenced "in all kinds of counterfeit miracles, signs and wonders, and in every sort of evil that deceives those who are perishing" (2:9–10). But joy! "The Lord Jesus will overthrow [him] with the breath of his mouth and destroy [him] by the splendor of his coming" (2:8). And the Thessalonians and all others whom God has chosen to be "saved through the sanctifying work of the Spirit and through belief in the truth" (2:13) will "share in the glory of our Lord Jesus Christ" when He appears (2:14).

Paul's prayer is therefore appropriate: "May the Lord direct your hearts into God's love and Christ's perseverance" (3:5).

Do not be idle

As in his first letter (1 Thessalonians 4:11–12), Paul warns against idleness here. "Keep away from every brother who is idle" (2 Thessalonians 3:6). This admonition was prompted by reports that some of the believers were indeed idle—"not busy," but "busybodies" (3:11).

Paul cites his own industry as an example: "We were not idle when we were with you, nor did we eat anyone's food without paying for it. On the contrary, we worked night and day, laboring and toiling so that we would not be a burden to any of you. We did this . . . in order to make ourselves a model for you to follow" (3:7–9). He reminds them of the "rule" he gave them during his stay in Thessalonica: "'If a man will not work, he shall not eat'" (3:10).

Two benedictions (3:16, 18) and a greeting in Paul's own script conclude the letter.

Our knowledge of Christ's return has been extended considerably by Paul's two letters to the Thessalonians. We must await our survey of Revelation to learn substantially more.

Meanwhile, we will look next at the three so-called pastoral letters—First and Second Timothy and Titus—addressed to two of Paul's valued co-workers in the ministry.

"Second mile" questions and topics

1. In view of Christ's return, what are some of the specific ways we should be living?

2. What lessons do you see in these two letters concerning the Christian's attitude toward the death of a fellow believer (1 Thessalonians 4:13–14, 18)? Toward persecution and affliction (2 Thessalonians 1:4–7)? Toward work (1 Thessalonians 4:9–12; 2 Thessalonians 3:10–13)?

9

Messages to Younger Ministers
First and Second Timothy and Titus—also Philemon

Into the Word Each Day

1. 1 Timothy 2:1–8   First, prayer
2. 1 Timothy 6:6–12   Fight the good fight
3. 2 Timothy 2:1–10   Be strong; endure hardship
4. 2 Timothy 3:10–17   As for you, continue
5. Titus 2:1–8   Teach sound doctrine
6. Titus 3:1–8   God was merciful to us
7. Philemon 1–7   Actively share your faith

WE HAVE ALREADY EXAMINED three "prison letters"—letters Paul wrote to churches while he was in "chains" in Rome. Those three were Ephesians, Philippians and Colossians. We mentioned a fourth that we would look at in its regular sequence in the New Testament: Philemon. We intend to survey Philemon later in this chapter.

Actually one other of Paul's letters deserves the term "prison letter," for Second Timothy was also written while the apostle was incarcerated in Rome. But because it deals, as does First Timothy and Titus, with matters about the ministry, we know it and the other two as the "pastoral letters." As the titles imply, two of them are addressed to Timothy; the third, to Titus.

The term "pastoral letters" has been used to designate these three communications since the early 18th century, but be careful not to read your current concepts of "pastor," "clergy" and "the ministry" into first-century practice. The word "pastor," designating a calling or a church office, occurs only in Ephesians 4:11, where it is qualified by the word "teacher" and should be translated (in the plural) "pastor-teachers." Most certainly the role of the first-century "pastor" differed significantly from the role of today's pastor or minister.

We do not know for sure whether Paul underwent just one imprisonment at Rome (the one mentioned in Acts 28), or whether he was eventually freed and then was again imprisoned in Rome. That there may have been two imprisonments can be inferred by the tone of Paul's letters from prison to the Philippians and to Philemon. To the Philippians he talks about "deliverance" (1:19), and concludes that although he would rather be with Christ, he is convinced that he should "remain in the body" (1:24), and assures them he "will remain" and will be with them again (1:25–26). He asks Philemon to "prepare a guest room" for him; "I hope to be restored to you in answer to your prayers" (v. 22).

By contrast, in Second Timothy, Paul senses his death is near. "The time has come for my departure," he says in an evident reference to death (2 Timothy 4:6).

If there were two Rome imprisonments for Paul—and some scholars lean toward that view—then First Timothy was written in the interval after his first imprisonment, and Second Timothy was written during his later captivity, probably very shortly before his execution.

Titus probably falls within the time frame of First and Second Timothy.

The men to whom the letters were written

We know quite a bit about Timothy from the New Testament. He was from Lystra, a town in Asia Minor that Paul visited twice on his first mission (Acts 14:8–21), again on his second (Acts 16:1) and also probably on his third (Acts 19:22). Timothy's mother was a believing Jewess; his father, a Greek (Acts 16:1–3), whether a believer or not we do not know. He knew the Scriptures from childhood (2 Timothy 3:14–15).

Paul calls Timothy his "true son in the faith" (1 Timothy 1:2), by which we understand that he was one of Paul's converts, probably from Paul's initial contacts in Lystra. He was well-spoken of by the local believers (Acts 16:2). At Paul's request he joined the missionary team (Acts 16:3). Thereafter he was Paul's constant companion (Philippians 2:22)—a trusted and trustworthy co-worker (2:19–20).

For a time Timothy was overseer of the important church at Ephesus (1 Timothy 1:3). In the waning years of Paul's life, while imprisoned in Rome, he requested Timothy's presence (2 Timothy 4:9–11, 13). We do not know if Timothy reached Paul before the apostle died.

By contrast, we know almost nothing about Titus, and this is remarkable in view of the letter addressed to him. He is not mentioned in Acts. Paul calls him "my own son after the common faith" (Titus 1:4), leading us to believe that he, too, was a convert of the apostle. Assuming the reference in Galatians 2:1–3 is to the same Titus, he was a Greek, possibly from Antioch in Syria. He is mentioned in Second Corinthians 7, where he appears to be a trouble-shooter and emissary of the apostle (7:6–7, 13–15). He had a similar role in Crete at the time Paul wrote to him, "straighten[ing] out what was left unfinished and appoint[ing] elders in every town" as Paul had directed him (Titus 1:5).

First Timothy

Paul's first letter to Timothy has a double thrust. There is emphasis on Timothy as a person and an emphasis on Timothy's official responsibilities. The two themes are intertwined throughout the book.

Paul had given Timothy the job of seeing that the church at Ephesus remained stable. It was no small responsibility. There were false teachers preoccupied with "myths and endless genealogies" (1 Timothy 1:4). It was Timothy's task to see that these promoters of controversies desisted.

Paul is concerned that Timothy "fight the good fight, holding on to faith and a good conscience" (1:18–19). He is to "point . . . out to the brothers" (4:6) the goodness of everything in God's creation and the emptiness of "hypocritical" teachers who would "forbid people to marry" or to eat certain foods (4:3–4). Although still youthful, he is to "set an example for the believers in speech, in life, in love, in faith and in purity" (4:12). He is to "devote" himself "to the public reading of Scripture, to preaching and to teaching" (4:13). He is not to "neglect" the "gift" given him "through a prophetic message when the body of elders laid their hands" on him (4:14). He is to "watch [his] life and doctrine closely" (4:16).

Paul also exhorts Timothy to be impartial: "Do nothing out of favoritism" (5:21). He is to "keep [himself] pure" (5:22). He is to "flee" from the love of money (6:9–11) and rather "pursue righteousness, godliness, faith, love, endurance and gentleness" (6:11). He is to "fight the good fight of the faith" (6:12). He is to "guard what has been entrusted to [his] care," turning away from "godless chatter and the opposing ideas of what is falsely called knowledge" (6:20).

Timothy's official responsibilities

Not only does the letter emphasize the personal discipline and character that Paul feels is so essential for Timothy, but the apostle speaks about Timothy's official responsibilities as the representative of the apostle at Ephesus.

The first of these is prayer. "I urge, then, first of all," Paul says, "that requests, prayers, intercession and thanksgiving be made for everyone" (2:1). The petitions are to include "kings and all those in authority" and this for the practical purpose "that we may live peaceful and quiet lives in all godliness and holiness" (2:2). Those living under a Roman dictator would know how essential this exhortation was.

But prayer was not restricted to the pastor or the church at Ephesus. Paul says, "I want men everywhere to lift up holy hands in prayer" (2:8). Although Paul refers elsewhere to praying women, even to women praying publicly in the congregation (see 1 Corinthians 11:5,13), here he uses the word "men" in contrast to "women" (see 2:9–15).

In addition to his exhortation about praying, Paul instructed Timothy regarding certain "setting in order" (to borrow the phrase from Titus) of church affairs. These matters were five in number:

1. *Women's place and deportment in the church (2:9–12).* Women were to dress modestly, shunning expensive and excessive ornamentation in favor of good deeds "appropriate for women who profess to worship God." Women were to "learn in quietness and full submission." They were not "to teach or to have authority over a man." They were to "be silent."

2. *The qualifications of overseers (3:2–7).* Paul enumerates the qualifications of those who oversee the local church. These are to be men of probity: hospitable, gifted in teaching, seasoned in the faith.

The word here for overseer is *episkopos* or superintendent—

the term from which we get our word *bishop*. It refers not to a man over several churches but to a man, probably serving with several other men, over one congregation. *Overseer* seems to be used by Paul interchangeably with *presbyteros* or *elder*. Still a third word, *poimainein*—a verb—*to shepherd* or *to pastor*, is sometimes employed. For example, in Acts 20:28, where Paul is addressing the Ephesian church leaders, he says, "Guard yourselves and all the flock of which the Holy Spirit has made you overseers *(episkopos)*. Be shepherds *(poimainein)* of the church of God." And Peter says, "To the elders *(presbyteros)* among you, I appeal as a fellow elder *(sumpresbyteros)*, . . . be shepherds *(poimanate)* of God's flock" (1 Peter 5:1–2).

The probable explanation: No standard titles for church officials existed in the New Testament times. Certainly to *shepherd* visualizes the kind of concerned care these elders or bishops are to exercise.

In 5:17–20 Paul adds to what he has said about overseers, calling them elders in this instance. "The elders who direct the affairs of the church well are worthy of double honor, especially those whose work is preaching and teaching." Calling on an Old Testament command that forbids muzzling the ox while it is treading out the grain (Deuteronomy 25:4) and the words of Jesus to the 72 preachers He sent out (Luke 10:7), Paul firmly establishes the principle, " 'The worker deserves his wages.' " Although Paul himself forewent that privilege in order not to be a burden on new churches, these congregations were expected to compensate those who gave their time in ministry to them (cf. Galatians 6:6).

That principle must be tempered, however, by advice Paul imparts especially to Timothy. Financial gain should not be the motive for godliness (6:5). "People who want to get rich fall into temptation and a trap and into many foolish and harmful desires that plunge men into ruin and destruction.

. . . You, man of God, flee from all this" (6:9–11).

3. *The qualification of deacons (3:8–13).* Deacons must meet standards very similar to those for overseers. Their spiritual perception must be matched by a "clear conscience." Only after they are "tested" are they to serve.

4. *The status of widows (5:3–16).* Widows constituted still another classification within the church system. And not just any woman whose husband had died could qualify, but widows who were really in need. No official church assistance should go to widows who had children or grandchildren able to care for them. "If anyone does not provide for his relatives, and especially for his immediate family," Paul says, "he has denied the faith and is worse than an unbeliever."

To qualify for assistance, widows had to be "over sixty" and "well-known for [their] good deeds" (5:9–10). Paul advised younger widows to remarry.

5. *The slave-master relationship (6:1–2).* Timothy was to see that the slave-master relationship was what it should be. This became especially delicate when both were believers within the church. "Those who have believing masters are not to show less respect for them because they are brothers. Instead, they are to serve them even better, because those who benefit from their service are believers and dear to them."

A letter that has considerable to say about riches and money ends with a command to those who are wealthy. Wealth is uncertain; it does not deserve our trust. Our hope should be in "God, who richly provides us with everything for our enjoyment" (6:17). "Command [the rich] . . . to be rich in good deeds, and to be generous and willing to share. In this way they will lay up treasure for themselves as a firm foundation for the coming age, so that they may take hold of the life that is truly life" (6:18–19).

Second Timothy

If Paul was ultimately released from his first imprisonment in Rome and allowed to resume his itinerant missionary work, then Second Timothy, as we noted, was written while Paul was subsequently imprisoned in Rome, and probably very shortly before his death. (Tradition has Paul executed by the sword in A.D. 67 under Nero's persecution.) Paul looks back on a lifetime of courageous ministry with the satisfaction that he has "fought the good fight" and "finished [his] race" (4:7).

We approach Second Timothy with special reverence. We are hearing not only inspired Holy Scripture, but the dying words of a beloved warrior and by now a warm friend. The letter must have evoked in Timothy, Paul's son in the faith and partner in ministry, similar emotions, intensified by the bond of man-to-man fellowship between these two servants of the Lord.

Second Timothy is a letter of personal counsel, dictated with that mixture of seasoned wisdom and mortal urgency that characterize this elder statesman as he looks backward on his course and forward to the crown that awaits him. We can only briefly mention the points Paul makes:

- "Fan into flame the gift of God, which is in you through the laying on of my hands" (1:6; cf. 1 Timothy 4:14)
- "Do not be ashamed to testify about our Lord, . . . but join with me in suffering for the gospel" (1:8)
- "What you heard from me, keep as the pattern of sound teaching" (1:13)
- "Guard the good deposit that was entrusted to you" (1:14)
- "The things you have heard me say in the presence of many witnesses entrust to reliable men who will also be qualified to teach others" (2:2)
- "Do your best to present yourself to God as one approved, a workman who does not need to be ashamed and who correctly handles the word of truth" (2:15)

- "Flee the evil desires of youth, and pursue righteousness, faith, love and peace" (2:22)
- "Continue in what you have learned and have become convinced of" (3:14)
- "Preach the Word; be prepared in season and out of season; correct, rebuke and encourage—with great patience and careful instruction" (4:2)
- "Keep your head in all situations, endure hardship, do the work of an evangelist, discharge all the duties of your ministry" (4:5)

Six metaphors

In chapter 2 Paul employs six metaphors—seven if you include the inanimate "instrument" in 2:21—in his exhortation to young Timothy:
- As a *son*, Timothy is to be strong and diligent (2:1–2)
- As a *good soldier* of Jesus Christ, he is to endure hardship and please his commanding officer (2:3–4)
- As an *athlete*, he is to compete according to the rules (2:5)
- As a *hardworking farmer*, he is to receive a share of the crops (2:6)
- As a *workman*, he is to correctly handle the word of truth (2:15)
- As the Lord's *servant*, he is to be peaceable and kind to everyone, able to teach, unresentful (2:24)

One of the classic statements concerning the inspiration of Scripture is in Second Timothy: "All Scripture is God-breathed and is useful for teaching, rebuking, correcting and training in righteousness, so that the man of God may be thoroughly equipped for every good work" (3:16).

Last will and testament

Paul, the aged prisoner, all alone except for Luke, expresses a great desire to see Timothy once more (4:9). He hopes Timothy can arrive before winter (4:21). We already know from 4:13 one reason for the urgency: Paul needs his "cloak that [he] left with Carpus at Troas"—needs it against the damp chill of a Roman prison in the winter. But Paul has other requests: "Get Mark and bring him with you, because he is helpful to me in my ministry" (4:11)—Mark, the young nephew of Barnabas whom Paul refused to take on his second mission because he had left them in the middle of the first (Acts 15:36–40). But now Mark is helpful. How beautiful to know that Paul is willing to forgive and forget.

Paul also asks for his "scrolls, especially the parchments" (4:13). Presumably these may have been portions of the Scriptures. We cannot know. But the request says something about Paul. To the very end he was alert, inquisitive, studious. That also is beautiful.

How does a faithful servant of the Lord regard his life as he looks back upon the trials and difficulties he has been through, and forward to what lies ahead? Paul says, "I have fought the good fight, I have finished the race, I have kept the faith. Now there is in store for me the crown of righteousness, which the Lord, the righteous Judge, will award to me on that day—and not only to me, but also to all who have longed for his appearing" (4:7–8). That kind of satisfaction is priceless.

Did Timothy reach the side of his aged mentor? We do not know. Let us hope that he did—with John Mark and the parchments and the cloak.

Titus

The theme of Paul's brief letter to Titus is holistic ("healthful") doctrine. He mentions it in 1:9 and 2:1 and in three other phrases speaks of being "sound in the faith" (1:13), "sound in faith" (2:2) and of "soundness of speech" (2:8).

The letter is similar in content to First Timothy, but it is briefer. To Titus, for instance, Paul mentions only the qualifications of elders (1:7–9).

The letter to Titus contains two important doctrinal passages. The first is in chapter 2: "For the grace of God that brings salvation has appeared to all men. It teaches us to say" no "to ungodliness and worldly passions, and to live self-controlled, upright and godly lives in this present age, while we wait for the blessed hope—the glorious appearing of our great God and Savior, Jesus Christ, who gave himself for us to redeem us from all wickedness and to purify for himself a people that are his very own, eager to do what is good" (2:11–14).

The second also refers to the salvation provided us through Jesus Christ: "When the kindness and love of God our Savior appeared, he saved us, not because of righteous things we had done, but because of his mercy. He saved us through the washing of rebirth and renewal by the Holy Spirit, whom he poured out on us generously through Jesus Christ our Savior, so that, having been justified by his grace, we might become heirs having the hope of eternal life" (3:4–7).

Philemon

The brief, one-chapter letter to Philemon is also a prison letter, as we noted, likely written during Paul's initial two-year incarceration in Rome. It is a personal letter from one Christian to another.

Philemon was a citizen of Colossae, a well-to-do slave-owner. He was converted under Paul's ministry (v. 19). The church at Colossae met in his house (v. 2). One of his household slaves, Onesimus, had robbed Philemon and run away to Rome, where he had come under Paul's influence and been converted to Christ.

Onesimus's name means "useful," and Paul plays on that meaning. "Formerly he was useless to you, but now he has become useful both to you and to me" (v. 11). Paul would have liked to keep him, but he does not want to do anything without Philemon's consent (v. 14). Paul hopes that Onesimus will be received "no longer as a slave, but better than a slave, as a dear brother" (v. 16). Paul intercedes for Onesimus: "If he has done you any wrong or owes you anything, charge it to me. . . . I will pay it back" (vv. 18–19).

Recapitulation

We have had our last glimpse of Paul in the New Testament. Some Bible scholars believe Paul also wrote Hebrews (we will discuss that more fully in the next chapter), but if so, we see no glimpse of Paul himself in the writing.

Someone has said that if a line were stretched from Paul in the New Testament to Moses in the Old, only Jesus Christ would rise above the line. Truly Paul was a monumental figure. Not only is he still the greatest individual missionary in terms of work accomplished, but his 13 letters that are a part of our inspired Scriptures stand as a perpetual legacy of instruction, encouragement, admonition and blessing.

This former Pharisee and persecutor, to whom Jesus appeared "as to one abnormally born" (1 Corinthians 15:8), admits that he "worked harder than all" the other apostles. "Yet," he says, it was "not I, but the grace of God that was with me" (1 Corinthians 15:10). Personal efforts or grace of God, Paul has left us an example of industry, fervor, devotion and love that has never been duplicated.

"Second mile" questions and topics

1. List the qualifications for leaders enumerated by Paul in 1 Timothy 3:1–13. Does Titus 1:7–9 add anything more?

2. Second Timothy 2:11–13 may have been a song used in the first-century church. What does it say about Jesus? What does it say about us?

3. It troubles some people today that Paul (and the inspired letter to Philemon—now a part of sacred Scripture) should accept the concept of slavery with such apparent approval. Does that fact give us license to approve slavery today? Why, or why not?

10

Relating God's Old Testament to the New
Hebrews

Into the Word Each Day

1.	Hebrews 1:5–12	God speaks about His Son
2.	Hebrews 3:12–19	"'Do not harden your hearts'"
3.	Hebrews 7:11–17	A new order of priest
4.	Hebrews 8:1–6	The ultimate high priest
5.	Hebrews 11:1–10	The faith models
6.	Hebrews 12:18–25	A new holy mountain
7.	Hebrews 13:11–16	Our sacrifice: praise

IT IS HARD FOR US TO REALIZE that when Paul said to Timothy, "Devote yourself to the public reading of Scripture" (1 Timothy 4:13; cf. 2 Timothy 3:16), the only Bible Timothy had to read was the Old Testament. The earliest manuscripts of the New Testament were just then being developed.

Paul considered the Old Testament vitally important to the Christians in the young churches he had founded, including Timothy's congregation at Ephesus. For Gentile believers, the Old Testament provided a base for understanding the gospel of Jesus Christ that their faith had embraced.

But turn that situation around. Here are Jews steeped in all the Old Testament tradition and Law-keeping. They put their faith in Jesus Christ. No wonder there were Judaizers who insisted that even Gentile Christians should keep the Old Testament Law. They could not disassociate Christianity from their spiritual roots. The transition from Law to grace was a long leap.

Hebrews, more than any other New Testament book, seeks to bridge that gap.

Who wrote Hebrews?

Tantalizingly, we do not know who wrote Hebrews. Some of the early traditions attribute it to Paul, but it is written in a style different from any of the Pauline letters. The earliest tradition admits the author is "known only to God." It is safest to leave it at that.

The anonymous author was a brilliant person, certainly a Jew totally familiar with the Old Testament, but also a devout Christian whose relationship to Jesus Christ is unquestioned. Not even Romans is as well-organized or as meticulous in its development.

We do not know the author, and we have only a few small hints as to who the first recipients were. That they were a specific church congregation seems clear by verses such as Hebrews 10:25, where the readers are told not to give up "meeting together," and in 10:32–34, where the writer reminds them of the early days when they were "publicly exposed to insult and persecution." They could hardly have been the church in Jerusalem, for the writer says, "In your struggle against sin, you have not yet resisted to the point of shedding your blood" (12:4). The Jerusalem church early had martyrs (see Acts 7:59–60; 12:1–2).

Hebrews 13:24 drops an innocuous hint: "Those from Italy send you their greetings." The preposition is *apo*—those *out from* Italy send greetings. Send greetings where? Back home to Italy is the implication. Perhaps this letter was primarily addressed to Jewish believers in the Imperial City. That would also account for their familiarity with Timothy (13:23), who had been in Rome while Paul was a prisoner there. It would also explain why the first known reference to this letter was by Clement of Rome.

Internal evidence also helps us fix the date of its composition. It could not have been early, for the gospel had been among them for some years (cf. 2:3 and 5:12). On the other hand, it must have been written before A.D. 70 when the Temple was destroyed, for the writer speaks as if the Temple and its furnishings were yet in place. A date between A.D. 64 and 67 is likely.

More so than with most of the other New Testament books, Hebrews is thematic. These several themes are interwoven throughout the letter, and an understanding of Hebrews is only possible as these themes are recognized and examined.

The speaking theme

The first and by far the most prominent theme is set forth in the opening sentence of Hebrews: "In the past God spoke to our forefathers through the prophets at many times and in various ways, but in these last days he has spoken to us by his Son, whom he appointed heir of all things, and through whom he made the universe" (1:1–2). Stripped of all but its basic elements it reads, "God spoke," and "he has spoken." God "has spoken to us by his Son." That is the underlying message of the entire letter.

Speaking by His Son was not God's first time to address His creation. In Old Testament times He spoke through the prophets. They were His mediums for conveying His message to mankind: Moses, Samuel, Elijah, Isaiah and many others.

But now God has spoken again—this time by His Son. Jesus

was more than just another prophet, more than just another mouthpiece. Jesus was Himself God. Not only what He said but His very life was a part of the message, and that is why it is so important that we steep ourselves in the New Testament Gospels as well as the apostolic letters such as the ones we have been examining.

If God has spoken by His Son, we need to "pay more careful attention . . . to what we have heard, so that we do not drift away" (2:1). "Therefore, . . . fix your thoughts on Jesus" (3:1).

> *"Today, if you hear his voice,*
> *do not harden your hearts*
> *as you did in the rebellion,*
> *during the time of testing in the desert,*
> *where your fathers tested and tried me*
> *and for forty years saw what I did.*
> *That is why I was angry with that generation,*
> *and I said, 'Their hearts are always going astray,*
> *and they have not known my ways.'*
> *So I declared on oath in my anger,*
> *'They shall never enter my rest.'"*
>
> Hebrews 3:7–11

It is hard for us, reading the Old Testament books of Exodus and Numbers, to understand how the children of Israel could have been so deaf to God's voice and so disobedient to His commands. But the writer reminds us that in this Christian era we can be just as guilty of ignoring the speaking God. He urges us to "make every effort to enter that rest, so that no one will fall by following their example of disobedience" (4:11).

And then the author has something to say about the Word of God: "The word of God is living and active. Sharper than any double-edged sword, it penetrates even to dividing soul and spirit, joints and marrow; it judges the thoughts and attitudes of the heart" (4:12). The reference may be to the written Word, the Bible. It may also be a reference to the Living Word, Jesus Christ Himself. Before Him "everything is uncovered and laid bare" and to Him "we must give account" (4:13).

A priest after Melchizedek

This Word is a heavenly high priest (4:14), but not after the Levitical line of priests "unable to sympathize with our weaknesses" (4:15). Rather, Jesus is a priest after the Melchizedek order (5:6).

What does a priest do? He *intercedes*. And Jesus interceded for us, "offer[ing] up prayers and petitions with loud cries and tears to the one who could save him from [literally *out from*] death" (5:7). And so "he became the source of eternal salvation for all who obey him" (5:9). And the writer is anxious that his readers be among that number: "We . . . want you . . . to imitate those who through faith and patience inherit what has been promised" (6:12).

The writer lingers on that spoken promise of salvation. He continues, "Because God wanted to make the unchanging nature of his purpose very clear to the heirs of what was promised, he confirmed it with an oath. God did this so that, by two unchangeable things in which it is impossible for God to lie, we who have fled to take hold of the hope offered to us may be greatly encouraged" (6:17–18).

Philip Mauro describes the anchor rocks imbedded in the ground at water's edge in the Mediterranean harbors of Bible times. They served as moorings for the little boats, but they had a secondary purpose. If a ship by means of its sails could not make the harbor, a sailor would row ashore in a dinghy, trailing a line which he would make fast to the anchor rock.

Those on the ship then had only to hold fast to the line and by patient effort pull themselves into the safety of the harbor.

The writer of Hebrews says of God's promised salvation: "We have this hope as an anchor for the soul, firm and secure. It enters the inner sanctuary behind the curtain, where Jesus, who went before us, has entered on our behalf" (6:19–20).

Who was Melchizedek?

Four times Jesus is called a priest "in the order of Melchizedek" (5:6; 5:10; 6:20; 7:17). Who was Melchizedek?

He appears briefly on the Old Testament scene (Genesis 14:18–20) as Abram (later renamed Abraham) returned from defeating the four kings who had carried off his nephew. He is called "king of Salem [Jerusalem]" and "priest of God Most High." After he pronounced a blessing upon Abram, "Abram gave him a tenth of everything." That and an even briefer reference to Melchizedek in Psalm 110:4 are the only mentions of him in the Old Testament.

His name means "king of righteousness," and "Salem" is the Hebrew for *peace* (Hebrews 7:2). The very absence of data concerning his birth, parentage and death makes him an especially appropriate symbol for the eternal Jesus Christ, who "remains a priest forever" (7:3). This permanence enables Him "to save completely those who come to God through him, because he always lives to intercede for them" (7:25).

A new covenant

Not only do we have a High Priest speaking intercession for us, but God pronounces a new covenant. The first covenant, based on laws and regulations that the children of Israel found themselves powerless to obey fully, has been superceded by another promised by God through the prophet Jeremiah (Jeremiah 31:33–34):

> "This is the covenant I will make with
>   the house of Israel after that time, declares the Lord.
> I will put my laws in their minds
>   and write them on their hearts. . . .
> I will forgive their wickedness
>   and will remember their sins no more"
>
> Hebrews 8:10–12.

The old covenant was specifically the Ten Commandments (see 9:4, and compare it with Exodus 34:28). The Ten Commandments were couched for the most part in negative terms: "You shall not, you shall not, you shall not." The new covenant is positive: "I will, I will, I will." God promises to do for us what we were powerless to do for ourselves.

And because God has spoken to us a new and better covenant, we are to speak to one another words of encouragement: "Let us not give up meeting together, as some are in the habit of doing, but let us encourage one another—and all the more as you see the Day approaching" (10:25). One of the important reasons for the worshipful gathering of Christians is the mutual encouragement we can be to each other.

Faith is believing what God says

Even the celebrated "faith chapter"—Hebrews 11—is premised on the speaking God. Faith is described as "being sure of what we hope for and certain of what we do not see" (11:1). "Without faith it is impossible to please God, because anyone who comes to him must believe that he exists and that he rewards those who earnestly seek him" (11:6).

But what is faith? Three of the examples used by the author

of Hebrews will give us a definition. "By faith Noah . . . built an ark" (11:7). "By faith Abraham, even though he was past age . . . was enabled to become a father" (11:11). "By faith Abraham . . . offered Isaac as a sacrifice" (11:17). An examination of the accounts in the book of Genesis makes it clear that in each case God had spoken—He had commanded. To Noah God said, " 'Make yourself an ark' " (Genesis 6:14). God said to the elderly Abraham, " 'A son coming from your own body will be your heir' " (15:4). And again, " 'Take your son, your only son Isaac, whom you love, and go to the region of Moriah. Sacrifice him there' " (22:2). God spoke. Noah and Abraham obeyed. And Hebrews says "by faith" they did what they did. *Faith is believing what God says—and acting on it.*

The speaking theme continues

In chapter 12 of Hebrews the writer speaks: "Let us run with perseverance the race marked out for us" (12:2). "Let us fix our eyes on Jesus, the author and perfecter of our faith" (12:2). "Endure hardship as discipline" (12:7). "Make every effort to live in peace with all men and to be holy" (12:14). "See to it that no one misses the grace of God and that no bitter root grows up to cause trouble and defile many" (12:15). "See that no one is sexually immoral, or is godless like Esau" (12:16).

The writer says, "You have not come to a mountain that can be touched and that is burning with fire" (12:18)—a reference to Mount Sinai, where the Old Testament Law was spoken by God to Moses. "But you have come to Mount Zion, to the heavenly Jerusalem, the city of the living God. You have come to thousands upon thousands of angels in joyful assembly, to the church of the firstborn, whose names are written in heaven. You have come to God, the judge of all men, to the spirits of righteous men made perfect, to Jesus the mediator of a new covenant, and to the sprinkled blood that [note the expression] speaks a better word than the blood of Abel" (12:22–24).

"See to it that you do not refuse him who speaks" (12:25). His voice shook the earth from Sinai (12:26), but He has promised to shake not only earth but the heavens (12:26; Haggai 2:6).

This obligates us to one continuous spoken sacrifice: "Through Jesus, therefore, let us continually offer to God a sacrifice of praise—the fruit of lips that confess his name" (13:15).

The "falling away" theme

We have followed in some detail the speaking theme through Hebrews. Another theme, persistent if not as prominent, is the "falling away" theme, named after the expression "fall away" in Hebrews 6:6.

In Hebrews 2:1 the word is "drift away," and the image is of a boat or ship silently, imperceptibly drifting from where it was supposed to be. The writer is concerned lest his readers with that same ease drift away from the message of Christ they have received: "We must pay more careful attention, therefore, to what we have heard, so that we do not drift away" (2:1).

It is a concern that crops up frequently in the letter. In chapters 3 and 4 the writer three times quotes a warning from Psalm 95: "Do not harden your hearts as you did in the rebellion"— a reference to the days in the wilderness following the Exodus when Israel refused to believe that God who had delivered them miraculously from Egypt could lead them successfully into the promised land of Canaan.

In chapter 6 and again in chapter 10 the writer avows that those who "fall away" once they have been "enlightened," have "tasted the heavenly gift," have "shared in the Holy Spirit," have "tasted the goodness of the word of God and the powers of the coming age," cannot be "brought back to repentance, because to their loss they are crucifying the Son of God all over again and subjecting him to public disgrace" (6:4–6). A similar statement is in 10:26–31.

Despite the dire warnings of these two passages, both are immediately followed by words of encouragement: "Even though we speak like this, dear friends, we are confident of better things in your case—things that accompany salvation" (6:9), and "Do not throw away your confidence; it will be richly rewarded" (10:35).

Again in chapter 12, we find the warning, "See to it that you do not refuse him who speaks. If they did not escape when they refused him who warned them on earth, how much less will we, if we turn away from him who warns us from heaven?" (12:25).

The faith theme

We have already looked at parts of chapter 11 with its emphasis on faith. Faith is believing what God says—and acting on it. Israel could not enter the promised land because of her lack of faith (3:19), which in the preceding sentence is called disobedience.

The Hebrew Christians to whom this letter was addressed were to "hold firmly to the faith" they professed (4:14). It was "through faith and patience" that they would "inherit what has been promised" (6:12). They are reminded of God's word through the prophet Habakkuk that His "righteous one will live by faith" (10:38). They are to "fix [their] eyes on Jesus, the author and perfecter of [their] faith" (12:2).

The High Priest theme

Finally, there are the recurring references to Jesus the High Priest (see 4:14 mentioned above). Jesus came from the family of Judah, not the priestly family of Levi (7:13–14). But Jesus' High Priesthood was perfectly logical. He was not a Priest after the order of the Levites since there were Levitical priests already functioning (8:4); He was a Priest after the order of Melchizedek.

Even as high priests were "called by God" (5:4), so Jesus was called by God (5:5–6). Even as the Levitical priests offered sacrifices for the sins of the people (5:1), so Jesus offered "his own blood" (9:12) in a tabernacle not man-made (9:11) "having obtained eternal redemption" (9:12). This was a once-for-all offering (9:25), and when He reappears, it will be "bring[ing] salvation to those who are waiting for him" (9:28).

Having such "a great priest over the house of God," we are to "draw near to God with a sincere heart in full assurance of faith" (10:21–22).

Conclusion

Like many of the other letters we have examined, this one also closes with a number of practical exhortations:
  - "Keep on loving each other as brothers" (13:1)
  - "Do not forget to entertain strangers" (13:2)
  - "Remember those in prison . . . and those who are mistreated" (13:3)—probably referring to Christians so suffering for the faith
  - "Marriage should be honored by all, and the marriage bed kept pure" (13:4)
  - "Keep your lives free from the love of money and be content with what you have" (13:5)
  - "Remember your leaders. . . . Consider the outcome of

their way of life and imitate their faith" (13:7)

- "Do not be carried away by all kinds of strange teachings" (13:9)
- "Let us . . . bear the disgrace [Jesus] bore" (13:13)
- "Let us continually offer to God a sacrifice of praise" (13:15)
- "Do not forget to do good and to share with others" (13:16)
- "Obey your leaders and submit to their authority" (13:17) —a reference probably to leaders (cf. 13:7) in the church
- "Pray for us" (13:18)—meaning the writer, whoever he may have been, and his associates in the ministry

The benediction is especially meaningful:

"May the God of peace, who through the blood of the eternal covenant brought back from the dead our Lord Jesus, that great Shepherd of the sheep, equip you with everything good for doing his will, and may he work in us what is pleasing to him, through Jesus Christ, to whom be glory for ever and ever. Amen" (13:20–21).

"Second mile" questions and topics

1. Sapher observes that Hebrews 1:2–3 takes us to the end of history, to the beginning of history, before history began, and throughout history. Find the phrases that denote these eras.

2. Hebrews 11:1–35a is a glittering recital of "success" stories through faith. In the middle of verse 35 the tone dramatically changes. How do you reconcile that these "others" were tortured, imprisoned, killed? They, too, were people of faith (11:39).

11

Practical Words
James, First and Second Peter

Into the Word Each Day

1. James 1:12–18   God gives good gifts
2. James 3:2–12   The untamed tongue
3. James 5:13–18   The prayer of faith
4. 1 Peter 2:11–17   Live good lives
5. 1 Peter 3:13–22   Do good
6. 2 Peter 1:2–8   Building blocks for growth
7. 2 Peter 3:3–13   Jesus *is* coming

THE LETTERS OF JAMES AND PETER are three of the eight so-called general letters in the New Testament. They were called that because no church or individual is named as the addressee (Third John is an exception), not because they were necessarily circular like Ephesians.

Hebrews, the first of the general letters, carries no address or salutation, although, as we have already noted, it seems to have been intended for a specific congregation familiar to the writer. James was written "to the twelve tribes scattered among the nations" (1:1)—and that is about as general as a person can be when referring to believing Jews. First Peter was written "to God's elect [a term applied to the Jews] . . . throughout Pontus, Galatia, Cappadocia, Asia and Bithynia. Second

Peter is equally indefinite as to the addressees: "To those who through the righteousness of our God and Savior Jesus Christ have received a faith as precious as ours" (1:1).

When we get to First John in our next chapter, we will see that it bears no salutation. Second John is addressed to "the chosen lady and her children"—people, John says, "whom I love in the truth" (v. 1). Presumably he is referring to a woman and her children or to a woman leading a congregation, but he could be using the term figuratively to refer to a church congregation and its satellite churches. Third John is addressed to John's friend Gaius—someone, he declares, "whom I love in the truth" (v. 1). Jude is directed "to those who have been called, who are loved by God the Father and kept by Jesus Christ" (v. 1).

Which James?

The name James was quite common in early Christianity and in Judaism, deriving as it does from 'Jacob,' one of Judaism's three 'Great' patriarchs. There are at least three Jameses mentioned in the New Testament, two of them among the twelve apostles. Which of the three wrote the letter by that name? Only by deciding which ones did *not* write it can we determine which one did!

Neither of the two apostles named James was likely the writer. For one thing, they would probably have mentioned their apostleship. For another, the better known of the two, James the brother of John, was by this time dead, having been put to death by Herod the king probably in A.D. 44 (see Acts 12:1–2).

Much more likely the writer of the letter was Jesus' half-brother, mentioned among other passages in Matthew 13:55 and Mark 6:3. He seems not to have been a believer during Jesus' years in the flesh (see John 7:5), but after Jesus' resurrection Luke calls him a believer (Acts 1:14), probably as a result of his having seen Jesus alive after the crucifixion (1 Corinthians 15:7).

James, Jesus' half-brother, rather quickly became one of the recognized leaders of the Jerusalem church (Galatians 2:12) and was the spokesman at the Jerusalem church council (Acts 15:13) when the issue of Gentile converts and their relation to Jewish Law was debated and determined. He received Paul upon his return from his third mission (21:18). He was counted among the apostles (Galatians 1:19) although he was not one of the original 12.

Eusebius, one of the later church fathers (fourth century), says James was surnamed "the Just" because of his eminent virtue. It is also said that he bore the nickname "Camel Knees" because he spent so much time on his knees in prayer. He is not mentioned after the events of Acts 21:18. Tradition has him martyred in Jerusalem in A.D. 62.

The letter of James

James addresses his letter to Christian Jews outside Palestine (1:1). Its purpose seems to have been to strengthen believing Jews in the midst of suffering and persecution. The writing is intensely practical. It has no particular order or progression; each thought is a springboard to the next. We will therefore simply look at some of the topics in succession.

The first of these is the Christian attitude toward trials. James says, "Consider it pure joy, my brothers, whenever you face trials of many kinds, because you know that the testing of your faith develops perseverance" (1:2–3). This theme is suggested again in 5:7: "Be patient, then, brothers, until the Lord's coming." James refers to "the prophets" and Job as examples of "patience in the face of suffering" (5:10) and says, "We consider blessed those who have persevered" (5:11).

Wisdom is a second theme: "If any of you lacks wisdom, he should ask God, . . . and it will be given to him" (1:5). In 3:13–17 the wisdom theme is continued: Wisdom should be evidenced by a well-lived life and humble deeds of mercy toward the needy (cf. 1:26–27). There is a false wisdom, earthly, devilish; James would make sure his readers have "the wisdom that comes from heaven." It is "pure; . . . peace loving, considerate, submissive, full of mercy and good fruit, impartial and sincere."

"You rich people, weep and wail"

A brief reference to "the one who is rich" in 1:9–10 introduces a third theme that James deals with in greater length in chapters 2 and 5. In 2:1–9 he rebukes the discrimination that shows deference to the rich and puts down the impoverished. Keeping the "royal law found in Scripture, 'Love your neighbor as yourself,'" is a cure for such favoritism. Abraham and Rahab are presented as examples of those who showed concern for the needy (2:14–26).

In 5:1–6 James directs his remarks to the unbelieving rich and promises them "misery" ahead. "You have hoarded wealth in the last days. Look! The wages you failed to pay the workmen . . . are crying out against you. . . . You have lived on earth in luxury and self-indulgence."

A fourth theme is the tongue, first mentioned in 1:26, where James warns the "religious" person to "keep a tight rein on his tongue." He takes up the theme again in 3:2–12, taking pains to stress the world of mischief the tongue is capable of. Later he admonishes against slandering one another (4:11), an activity of the tongue.

The fifth theme we will touch on is Law-keeping (2:8–11). James says, "If you really keep the royal law found in Scripture, 'Love your neighbor as yourself,' you are doing right. But if you show favoritism, you sin and are convicted by the law as lawbreakers." Keeping the Law only counts if a person keeps it all. The slander we just mentioned in 4:11 is, James says, a violation of the Law we are supposed to keep. "Anyone who speaks against his brother or judges him, speaks against the law and judges it."

"Is any one of you sick?"

James very clearly outlines the procedure believers are to follow when they are sick (5:14–16). The sick person is to "call the elders of the church to pray over him and anoint him with oil in the name of the Lord." He is to call. He is to call the church officials most likely to be available—the elders of the congregation. The oil, although it was looked upon as medicinal (the Good Samaritan poured oil and wine on the wounds of the injured Jew in Jesus' parable—see also Isaiah 1:6 and Jeremiah 8:22), is symbolic here. Not the oil but the "prayer offered in faith will make the sick person well; the Lord will raise him up."

Note the possible relation of sin to sickness: "If he has sinned, he will be forgiven. Therefore confess your sins to each other and pray for each other so that you may be healed."

James ends his letter with a reference to Elijah's prayers and a tacit exhortation to seek the fellow-Christian's spiritual welfare.

First Peter

Addressed to "God's elect, . . . scattered throughout [Asia Minor]" (1:1), First Peter was written to suffering Christians (4:12). Quite possibly they were feeling the effects of the Roman Emperor Nero's persecution. Peter's reference in 5:13, "She who is in Babylon, chosen together with you, sends you her greetings," could refer to the literal Babylon, but more likely is a code word for Rome. The letter probably was written about A.D. 65, shortly before Peter's death.

The term *diaspora*—dispersion or scattering—implies a Jewish readership. On the other hand, the writer's later statement about his readers' pre-Christian life of "detestable idolatry" (4:4) indicates a non-Jewish audience, for at this time in their national history Jews were not idolaters.

Hebrew or Gentile readers, note how many references Peter makes to suffering in the five short chapters:

- "Now for a little while you may have had to suffer grief in all kinds of trials" (1:6)
- "The sufferings of Christ and the glories that would follow" (1:11)
- "It is commendable if a man bears up under the pain of unjust suffering" (2:19)
- "If you suffer for doing good and you endure it, this is commendable before God" (2:20)
- "Christ suffered for you, leaving you an example, that you should follow in his steps" (2:21)
- "When [Jesus] suffered, he made no threats" (2:23)
- "Even if you should suffer for what is right, you are blessed" (3:14)
- "It is better, if it is God's will, to suffer for doing good than for doing evil" (3:17)
- "Since Christ suffered in his body, arm yourselves also with the same attitude, because he who has suffered in his body is done with sin" (4:1)
- "Do not be surprised at the painful trial you are suffering, as though something strange were happening to you" (4:2)
- "Rejoice that you participate in the sufferings of Christ, so that you may be overjoyed when his glory is revealed" (4:13)
- "If you suffer, it should not be as a murderer or thief or

any other kind of criminal, or even as a meddler" (4:15)
- "If you suffer as a Christian, do not be ashamed, but praise God that you bear that name" (4:16)
- "Those who suffer according to God's will should commit themselves to their faithful Creator and continue to do good" (4:19)
- "I . . . [am] a witness of Christ's sufferings" (5:1)
- "The God of all grace, who called you to his eternal glory in Christ, after you have suffered a little while, will himself restore you and make you strong, firm and steadfast" (5:10)

What has Peter said? He has said that suffering is the normal lot of the Christian. Christ, our example, suffered. Therefore, when we suffer we are identifying with Christ. In suffering we should commit ourselves to our faithful Creator and do good; God cares. We should resist Satan, who plays a role in Christians' suffering.

Suffering has purpose: he who suffers ceases from sin, and suffering is a means to perfection or completeness. When we suffer we should remember, as Christ did, that glory follows, and be patient, unashamed and joyful amid it. We should cast our care on God.

Second Peter

Peter's second letter differs considerably in style from his first. But the writer claims to be Peter (1:1): he recalls Jesus' transfiguration, an event that only three of the apostles witnessed (see Mark 9:2); and he calls this his "second letter."

Although the correspondence bears no salutation, Peter's statement about this being "my second letter to you" implies that it was intended for the same recipients as his first. And, as we noted above, the exact composition of Peter's audience is difficult to determine. But that need not lessen our spiritual profit from it.

"Knowledge" is the key word in Second Peter. "Grace and peace be yours in abundance through the knowledge of God and of Jesus our Lord" (1:2). God has made full provision against doctrinal error. Knowledge combats false teaching. This concern of Second Peter about false teaching will be evident, too, in the remaining four general letters that we will look at in our next chapter.

In chapter 1, Peter holds out the Word of God as the believers' bulwark against the corrupting influences of the world: "[God] has given us his very great and precious promises, so that through them you may participate in the divine nature and escape the corruption in the world caused by evil desires" (1:4).

He urges his readers ("Make every effort," he says) to add to faith

> goodness
> > knowledge
> > > self-control
> > > > perseverance
> > > > > godliness
> > > > > > brotherly kindness
> > > > > > > love (1:5–7).

"If you possess these qualities in increasing measure," Peter says, "they will keep you from being ineffective and unproductive in your knowledge of our Lord Jesus Christ" (1:8).

Peter avows that he and his associates in the ministry "did not follow cleverly invented stories when we told you about the power and coming of our Lord Jesus Christ" (1:16). Peter here makes the other major New Testament statement concerning the Scriptures (cf. 2 Timothy 3:16): "You must understand that no prophecy of Scripture came about by the prophet's own interpretation. For prophecy never had its origin in the will of man, but men spoke from God as they were carried along by the Holy Spirit" (1:20–21).

There were false prophets, there are false teachers

But just as there had been false prophets in Israel who lied to the people, so "there will be false teachers among you"—teachers who "will secretly introduce destructive heresies, even denying the sovereign Lord who bought them" (2:1). Greed (2:3) is a part of their motive—"they are experts in greed" (2:14). "Slaves of depravity" (2:19), they have "turn[ed] their backs on the sacred commandment that was passed on to them" (2:21). But "their destruction has not been sleeping" (2:3). "The Lord knows how to rescue godly men from trials and to hold the unrighteous for the day of judgment, while continuing their punishment" (2:9).

Peter calls up four illustrations to drive home his point that these false teachers will be punished: (1) the "angels when they sinned" (2:4), (2) the pre-Flood world of people (2:5), (3) Sodom and Gomorrah (2:6) and (4) Balaam, the prophet "who loved the wages of wickedness" (2:15).

Jesus' Second Coming will be God's vindication

Even the return of Christ will be scoffed at by those "following their own evil desires" (3:3). "They will say, 'Where is this "coming" he promised? Ever since our fathers died, everything goes on as it has since the beginning of creation'" (3:4).

But they forget that God does not reckon time as we do. His supposed slowness "in keeping his promise" is because He wants to give time for "everyone to come to repentance" (3:9). The "day of the Lord will come like a thief" (3:10). With a roar the heavens will disappear. The very "elements will be destroyed by fire, and the earth and everything in it will be laid bare" (3:10). But in keeping with God's promise, Peter adds, "We are looking forward to a new heaven and a new earth, the home of righteousness" (3:13).

Peter uses this awesome but blessed prospect to urge his readers to "be on . . . guard so that you may not be carried away by the error of lawless men and fall from your secure position" (3:17).

The letter concludes with a loving admonition and a doxology: "Grow in the grace and knowledge of our Lord and Savior Jesus Christ. To him be glory both now and forever! Amen" (3:18).

"Second mile" questions and topics

1. Some people (including Martin Luther!) have seen a discrepancy between James's teaching on the necessity of faith and works (James 3:14–26) and Paul's teaching that faith alone saves us (Romans 3:27–30). How would you reconcile these seemingly differing statements?

2. Peter has a beautiful passage about wives and husbands in First Peter 3:1–7. At the end of it, what does he imply regarding prayer?

3. Peter's "building blocks" to Christian maturity in Second Peter 1:5–8 offer an interesting sequence. How does "brotherly kindness" differ from "love"?

12

Contending for the Faith
First John, Second John, Third John and Jude

Into the Word Each Day

1.	1 John 1:5—2:2	God is light
2.	1 John 3:1–6	How great is God's love
3.	1 John 4:11–21	We should love one another
4.	2 John 4–9	Love is obedience
5.	3 John 2–11	Love is practical
6.	Jude 3–7	"Contend for the faith"
7.	Jude 17–25	A call to persevere

THE FOUR GENERAL LETTERS to which we address ourselves in this chapter are bound together by a common concern: false teachers had appeared in the apostolic churches, and both John and Jude are determined that truth shall prevail.

Were we grouping the New Testament books strictly by subject, another letter would have to be included with these four: Second Peter, which we considered in our last chapter. Not only is false teaching a prominent subject of Second Peter, but the book is strikingly similar to Jude in subject matter, even to the illustrations each writer uses to illuminate his points.

First John

Although the author nowhere specifically says he is John, one of the disciples in Jesus' inner circle, he leaves little doubt as to his true identity. The writer is an eyewitness of the life of Christ (1:1–3; 4:14) and the letter's content and style are similar to the Gospel of John.

Likely this shorter treatise was intended to be a companion to the Gospel. Probably it was written shortly after John completed his Gospel.

John wrote his Gospel so that readers might "believe that Jesus is the Christ, the Son of God, and that by believing [they might] have life in his name" (20:31). John wrote the first of his three letters to those "who believe in the name of the Son of God so that [they] may know that [they] have eternal life" (1 John 5:13). In short, the Gospel of John declares salvation; First John gives assurance of it.

There is no reference in First John to the Old Testament, an omission that leads us to guess that Gentiles, not Hebrew Christians, may have been the apostle's primary target audience. If, as tradition has it, John became the senior elder in the church at Ephesus, the immediate recipients may have been the members of that church. Our only biblical information of John following the Jerusalem church council is his own statement in the Revelation that he was exiled for a time on Patmos, a small island in the Aegean Sea off the Asia Minor coast.

Two errors

John writes in part to define the nature of Christ. In our survey of Colossians we briefly considered the gnostic heresy, a system of the divine and heavenly hierarchy that denied that the Christ was really a man and did not accord Him the full rank of Deity. Gnosticism spawned two other heresies: Docetism, the belief that Jesus only *appeared* or *seemed* to be a flesh-and-blood human being, and its counterpart, Cerinthianism (named after Cerinthus, who formulated it), the belief that Jesus was a flesh-and-blood human being, but was only temporarily indwelt by God.

John insists on Christ's humanity. He had seen Jesus with his own eyes. His hands had touched Jesus (1:1). He was no apparition. John says, "This is how you can recognize the Spirit of God: Every spirit that acknowledges that Jesus Christ has come in the flesh is from God, but every spirit that does not acknowledge Jesus is not from God" (4:2–3).

When Peter confessed that Jesus was " 'the Christ, the Son of the living God' " (Matthew 16:16), Jesus replied, " 'This was . . . revealed to you . . . by my Father in heaven' " (16:17). Likewise Paul declares, "No one can say, 'Jesus is Lord,' except by the Holy Spirit" (1 Corinthians 12:30). John is affirming what Jesus implies and Paul states: our embracing of the truth concerning Jesus Christ is only possible through God's Holy Spirit who leads us into truth. Or, to put it the other way, our acceptance of the truth that Jesus actually was enfleshed is proof that the Spirit of God indwells us.

But John, while insisting on Christ's humanity, insists just as vigorously on His deity. He declares Jesus to be God's Son (1:3; 2:22–23; 3:23; 4:15; 5:20). The two natures of Jesus— divine and human—uniquely set Him apart and made possible a sacrifice for sins that God considered once-for-all adequate.

Fellowship, a theme of First John

An underlying theme of this letter is fellowship. The word occurs first in 1:3: "We proclaim to you what we have seen and heard, so that you also may have fellowship with us."

Human, interpersonal fellowship is possible because of our common faith in Jesus Christ.

But John immediately adds, "Our fellowship is with the Father and with his Son, Jesus Christ."

Fellowship has prerequisites. "If we claim to have fellowship with [God] yet walk in the darkness, we lie and do not live by the truth. But if we walk in the light, as he is in the light, we have fellowship with one another, and the blood of Jesus, his Son, purifies us from every sin" (1:6–7). Our fellowship with God depends on our walking "in the light." And that also assures us that the blood of Christ will continue to purify us from every sin.

Although the word *fellowship* does not occur elsewhere in the letter, it is implicit. For example, obedience to Jesus' commands is the way to know Him (2:3). The person who claims to know Him while at the same time ignoring His commands "is a liar, and the truth is not in him" (2:4).

John singles out two particular commands, one positive, one negative, perhaps because they are so easily broken, perhaps because they are so necessary to fellowship: Love your neighbor, and love not the world. Concerning the first he says, "Whoever hates his brother is in the darkness and walks around in the darkness" (2:11). And concerning the other: "If anyone loves the world, the love of the Father is not in him" (2:15). John defines *world* as "the cravings of sinful man, the lust of his eyes and the boasting of what he has and does" (2:16). It is not just the created order, but covers a wide spectrum of activity opposed to God in Christ.

Not so rigid after all

If your reading of First John has been limited to the King James Version, you may have been struck—and troubled—by John's absolute statements. For instance, "Whosoever abideth in [Jesus] sinneth not: whosoever sinneth hath not seen him, neither known him" (3:6). Or, "Whosoever is born of God doth not commit sin; for his seed remaineth in him: and he cannot sin, because he is born of God" (3:9). Or, "Whosoever is born of God sinneth not" (5:18).

Statements like these can be disconcerting to a believer sincerely trying to walk with God but nevertheless aware that he or she has had an occasional lapse, doing what he should not have done or—equally condemning—failing to do what he should have done.

Contemporary versions such as the New International resolve this difficulty by a more careful rendering of the verb tenses. John did not in fact speak so absolutely as the King James translators would have us think. Rather, he is speaking of making a practice of sinning. As John takes pains to point out, "If anybody does sin, we have one who speaks to the Father in our defense—Jesus Christ, the Righteous One. He is the atoning sacrifice for our sins, and not only for ours but also for the sins of the whole world" (2:1–2).

Light, life and love

Three recurring words, alliterative in English, though not in Greek, constitute a theme for First John. They are *light* (1:5; 1:7; 2:9; 2:10), *life* (1:1; 1:2; 3:14; 5:11–12) and *love* (4:8–12; 4:16; 5:1–3).

God is light, absolute light. As we walk in the light, we have fellowship with all others who are walking in the light, and the blood of Jesus, God's Son, continues to cleanse us from every sin. So important is this aspect of fellowship that it becomes a litmus test of our walk in the light. If we are out of fellowship with our "brother" (John probably was using the term to refer to any other member of the body of Christ, whether male or female), we are not walking in the light after all. Rather, we are "still in the darkness" (2:9).

It is a beautiful and very appropriate example of how the spiritual and the practical fit together in the Christian life. The walk with Christ is an inner, mystical experience, but it also is a very practical, outward relationship with others who have likewise had the inner, mystical experience.

God is life. John says he saw it, touched it. It was enfleshed, but it was eternal God, a final statement (remember Hebrews 1:1–4 and 4:12–13?) that God was making to His creation. The incredible part of the message is that we, too, can have this eternal life—but only as we have the Son, for life is in Him. "He who has the Son has life; he who does not have the Son of God does not have life" (5:12).

And would you believe it? John comes right back again to our "brother" for outward proof as to whether we have life. "We know that we have passed from death to life, because we love our brothers. Anyone who does not love remains in death" (3:14).

God is love. God demonstrated His love by sending Jesus "that we might live through him" (4:9). That He would do this is the more amazing when we realize that He was not responding to some overture on our part. God loved us first.

Again, John relates this to our fellow believers. "Since God so loved us, we also ought to love one another" (4:11). "If we love each other, God lives in us and his love is made complete in us" (4:12). "Everyone who loves the father loves his child as well" (5:1).

There is a second test of our love for God: obedience. "This is love for God: to obey his commands" (5:3).

Light, life, love. The parameters of Christian experience. All three involve us in a faith experience with God through Jesus Christ; all three can be empirically tested by our attitude toward and relation to God's other family members.

Second John

Second—and Third—John, like Philemon that we looked at three chapters ago, are examples of personal correspondence of that era. Without a doubt Paul and John and other apostles penned a number of personal letters. These three have been preserved by the Holy Spirit for us as part of God's inspired Word.

The writer calls himself "the elder." We infer from the title that he was well-known by that identification. The elderly John, probably last remaining of the original 12 apostles, is the almost uncontested deduction.

Like Second Peter and First John, this letter is concerned with false teachers.

As we suggested earlier, "the chosen lady and her children" whom John loved in the truth (v. 1) may have been an individual and her family, or figurative language for a church congregation and its satellite groups.

The occasion of the letter was the apostle's discovery of some of her "children walking in the truth, just as the Father commanded us" (v. 4). John seizes on the occasion to reiterate some of what he said in First John about love to one another and obedience to God's commands (vv. 5–6). He also warns against "deceivers, who do not acknowledge Jesus Christ as coming in the flesh" (v. 7), and he says such teachers of falsehood are not to be shown hospitality (vv. 10–11).

Third John

John's third letter, to his "dear friend Gaius" (v. 1), is a letter of encouragement. John makes six references to "the truth" (vv. 1, 4, 8, 12) and commends Gaius for his hospitality to the traveling "brothers" (vv. 5–8).

In contrast is Diotrephes, who not only has gossiped "maliciously" about John but who "refuses to welcome the brothers" (vv. 9–10). Demetrius, on the other hand, "is well spoken of by everyone" (v. 12).

As in Second John, the apostle hopes soon to pay a visit to the recipient, in which face-to-face meeting he will convey the other matters on his mind and heart. The letter concludes with a brief benediction and greetings.

Jude

Jude, the author, identifies himself as "a servant of Jesus Christ and a brother of James" (v. 1). Probably he refers to James the well-known church leader and writer of the letter bearing that name. If so, Jude was a half-brother of Jesus (see Matthew 13:55; Mark 6:3) who came to faith sometime late in Jesus' public ministry or afterward.

He addresses his letter to "those who have been called, who are loved by God the Father and kept by Jesus Christ" (v. 1)—a very general designation. His references to Old Testament events, places and people seem to slant the letter especially to Hebrew Christians—possibly the same readership his brother James wrote to. The absence of any reference to the destruction of Jerusalem in A.D. 70 leads us to believe it was written before that date.

Jude, too, is concerned about false teachers.

As we noted, there is a close resemblance between Jude and the second and third chapters of Second Peter. Both writers bring scathing indictments against perverters of the truth. Both see the return of the Lord as the final rectifier of injustice and untruth. Note that Peter warns that false teachers *will come* (2 Peter 2:1). Jude says false teachers *now are here* (v. 4), an indication that Peter's letters predated the one by Jude.

Jude makes two specific references to extra-biblical information. In verse 9 he refers to Michael's disputation with the devil about the body of Moses—an incident, according to some of the early church fathers, found in a Jewish apocryphal book, no longer extant, known as *The Assumption of Moses*. He quotes a prophecy of Enoch (vv. 14–15) found not in the Bible but in a Jewish apocalypse entitled *The Book of Enoch*.

Rather than to call in question the validity of such information from non-inspired sources, we should assume the truthfulness of the statements because God influenced Jude to include them in this letter that is a part of the inspired Bible. The fact that the apocryphal books contain non-factual material does not mean that all the material within them is untrue.

Jude indicates that he has been forced by circumstances to write other than what he preferred to write. He says, "Although I was very eager to write to you about the salvation we share, I felt I had to write and urge you to contend for the faith that was once for all entrusted to the saints" (v. 3). So he begins with an exhortation to *defend the faith*.

This defense was against "godless men, who change the grace of our God into a license for immorality and deny Jesus Christ our only Sovereign and Lord" (v. 4)—an indication that error within the apostolic church was already full-blown.

Some have departed from the faith

This follows with illustrations of those who have *departed from the faith* (vv. 5–16). Israel was saved out of Egypt, but "those who did not believe" were destroyed in the wilderness (v. 5). The "angels who . . . abandoned their own home" are being "kept in darkness, bound with everlasting chains for judgment on the great Day" (v. 6)—possibly a reference to Genesis 6 and the later destruction of the antediluvian world.

Sodom and Gomorrah earned "the punishment of eternal fire" (v. 7).

The scathing indictment of verses 11–16 with its metaphorical language bares the depths of Jude's feelings about these perverters of the faith that was once for all entrusted to the saints.

The "way of Cain" (v. 11) was a willful savagery against his more-obedient brother (Genesis 4:3–8). "Balaam's error" was greed (note Numbers 22:17: " 'I will reward you handsomely' "). "Korah's rebellion" is a reference to Numbers 16:1–35, and the time when Korah and a company of 250 community leaders insolently defied Moses and Aaron's authority and died at God's hand.

Even as those Old Testament examples were judged and condemned, so for these godless men the "blackest darkness has been reserved forever" (v. 13).

Jude then turns to his readers. "You, dear friends, build yourselves up in your most holy faith and pray in the Holy Spirit. Keep yourselves in God's love as you wait for the mercy of our Lord Jesus Christ to bring you to eternal life" (vv. 20–21). He reminds them of apostolic teaching (vv. 17–18). He exhorts them to attempt to rescue those ensnared by false teachers—but with care. The letter closes with an optimistic doxology in praise of "him who is able to keep you from falling and to present you before his glorious presence without fault and with great joy" (v. 24).

"To the only God our Savior be glory, majesty, power and authority, through Jesus Christ our Lord, before all ages, now and forevermore! Amen" (v. 25).

Summary

We have concluded our survey of the general letters—Hebrews, James, Peter's two letters, John's three and Jude. We have seen how God used these men to warn, to fortify, to encourage. The circumstances and problems encountered by Christians of that apostolic era are little different from those we encounter yet today. The messages of these writers to first-century believers continue to be timely.

This chapter also concludes our look at all of the New Testament with the exception of one book—Revelation. Revelation is different in nature from any of the other New Testament books, and yet in a sense it incorporates elements of them all. We will see the Jesus of the Gospels glorified, exalted. We will look at brief messages (mini-letters) to seven churches of Asia Minor. And then the curtains will open on a great panorama of events as God lets us glimpse what is yet future, including the return of His Son, Jesus Christ, as World Conqueror and the new heavens and earth where God dwells with His redeemed creation.

"Second mile" questions and topics

1. In First John the writer tells us to "test the spirits." What do you think he means by this? Does Second John 7–10 throw any light on the subject? (Hint: 1 Corinthians 14:29 ff. and 1 Thessalonians 5:21–22 reflect similar practices.)

2. From the reference in Third John 5–8 about "the brothers," describe in your own words the kind of itinerant preaching that seems to have gone on in first century house churches.

3. Jude speaks of the error of Balaam (v. 1). Peter referred to "the way of Balaam" (2 Peter 2:15). In Revelation 2:14 there is mention of "the teaching of Balaam." We identified the error of Balaam as greed. Read Numbers 22—24, where the story of Balaam is recorded, and see if you can name the way of Balaam and the teaching of Balaam. (His death is mentioned in Joshua 13:22.)

13

The Finale That Is a Prelude
Revelation

Into the Word Each Day

1.	Revelation 1:4–8	The seven churches
2.	Revelation 3:14–21	One of the mini-letters
3.	Revelation 5:11–14	" 'Worthy is the Lamb!' "
4.	Revelation 13:1–8	The blasphemous beast
5.	Revelation 14:14–20	Earth's "harvest" is reaped
6.	Revelation 20:11–15	Judgment Day
7.	Revelation 21:1–7	A new heaven and earth

WE HAVE COME TO THE LAST book of the Holy Bible, the most thoroughly predictive piece of writing in the New Testament. As we come, a surprise awaits us. Revelation is not so much a conclusion to the New Testament and to the Bible as it is a preview of a wonderful new beginning.

The true title of the book is in the first five words: "The revelation of Jesus Christ." You may have heard the term "apocalypse" used in reference to Revelation. It is from a similar Greek word meaning "unveiling." Literally Revelation is the unveiling of Jesus Christ—the drawing back of the curtains so that we can see Him in all His splendor and majesty.

Simply John

The writer identifies himself in 1:1, 1:4, 1:9 and 22:8 as John. Only one person was well enough known to employ that name alone: John the apostle, writer of the Gospel according to John and writer of the three letters we examined in the previous chapter. The intended audience, "the seven churches in the province of Asia" (1:4), further substantiates John the apostle's authorship, for according to tradition John was long associated with the church in Ephesus.

At the time he wrote, John was in exile on Patmos, a rocky, isolated 4-mile-by-8-mile island off the coast of Asia Minor. He had been banished there "because of the Word of God and the testimony of Jesus" (1:9). Probably this was during the persecution under Domitian, A.D. 95.

In broadest outline the book has two divisions. The first, chapters 1—3, is concerned with the seven named churches of Asia Minor: Ephesus, Smyrna, Pergamum, Thyatira, Sardis, Philadelphia and Laodicea (1:11). The second, beginning with chapter 4 and the heavenly throne room, takes us all the way to the new heavens and earth (21:1) and to the New Jerusalem (21:2). Revelation, incidentally, is the only book of the Bible that promises a blessing to those who read it (1:3).

The Revelation centers around four visions that John saw while in exile, the first being of "someone 'like a son of man'" (1:13) among "seven golden lampstands" (1:12), holding in his right hand seven stars (1:16). This awesome Person identifies Himself as "'The first and the last, . . . the Living One [who] was dead, [but who is] alive for ever and ever!'" Clearly He is Jesus Christ. Jesus also identifies the seven stars as the "'angels of the seven churches'" and the lampstands as the seven churches (1:20).

He commands John to "'write'" (1:19), and the way He puts it suggests the perspective of this prophetic book. "'Write

. . . what you have seen, what is now and what will take place later' " (1:19). "What you have seen" was the vision John had just witnessed of Jesus Christ. "What is now" refers to the several messages given to the seven churches (chapters 2 and 3). "What will take place later" denotes the visions beginning with chapter 4 and going on to the end of the book.

Although that part of Revelation was clearly future at the time John wrote in the last years of the first century, the question is legitimate as to whether all of it is still future. In 1,900 years of history some of it could have taken place. The strongest argument for believing the predictions are still future, to be fulfilled in a comparatively short segment of time near to the Lord's return to earth, is a practical one: it is not possible to match the predictions with known historical events in the world.

The messages to the seven churches

Jesus addresses Himself through John to each of the "angels" (messengers—possibly leaders) of the named churches, describing Himself in every case in terms of the revelation He showed John (1:12–18). For example, to the angel of the church at Ephesus He calls Himself " 'him who holds the seven stars in his right hand and walks among the seven golden lampstands' " (2:1).

Jesus lays a charge against five of the seven churches, the exceptions being Smyrna and Philadelphia. The Ephesians had forsaken their " 'first love' " (2:4); the church in Pergamum harbored false teachers (2:14–15); the Thyatira church tolerated a misleading prophetess; the church in Sardis was " 'dead' " (3:1); the Laodicea church was lukewarm (3:15).

For each Jesus voices a precept to follow. For four of the seven that precept was to repent.

For each church Jesus also makes a promise to those who " 'overcome' " (2:7, 11, 17, 26; 3:5, 12, 21).

" 'What must take place after this' "

This brings us to the future vision—actually to three future visions, each introduced by the phrase, "I was in the Spirit" (4:2; 17:3; 21:10). In the first, John hears a "voice . . . speaking to [him] like a trumpet" (4:1). He is immediately ushered into the heavenly throne room of awesome splendor and perpetual praise.

As John begins to take in details, he sees a scroll in the "right hand of him who sat on the throne" (5:1). It is sealed with seven seals. When no one is found who can break the seven seals, "a Lamb, looking as if it had been slain" (5:6), takes the scroll.

The seals are broken

As the slain-but-living Lamb breaks one seal after another, we see identifiable calamities:
- A white horse—conquest without war (6:2)
- A red horse—war (6:4)
- A black horse—famine (6:5–6)
- A pale horse—death "by sword, famine and plague, and by the wild beasts of the earth" (6:8)
- "The souls of those who had been slain because of the word of God and the testimony they had maintained" (6:9)
- A great earthquake, stellar disturbances, dislocated mountains and islands (6:12–14)

Before the seventh seal is broken, we have an interlude: the sealing of 144,000 "from all the Tribes of Israel" (7:1–8), and the presence in heaven of "a great multitude that no one could count, from every nation, tribe, people and language," who cry loudly:

> *"Salvation belongs to our God,*
> *who sits on the throne,*
> *and to the Lamb"*
> *7:10.*

These are identified as "'they who have come out of the great tribulation'" (7:14).

The trumpet judgments

The seventh seal ushers in a series of "trumpet" judgments, called that because each is preceded by an angel's sounding of a trumpet he holds.

1. Hail and fire mixed with blood is hurled down upon the earth, burning up a third of the earth, a third of the trees and all the green grass (8:7).

2. Something like a huge, blazing mountain, landing in the sea, turns a third of the sea into blood. A third of the sea life dies, and a third of the shipping is destroyed (8:8–9).

3. A great, blazing star strikes a third of the rivers and springs of water, turning the water bitter and lethal (8:10–11).

4. A third of the sun, moon and stars are "struck . . . so that a third of them turned dark," a third of the day and night are without light (8:12).

5. A fallen star is "given the key to the shaft of the Abyss." He opens the shaft and smoke rises as from a gigantic furnace, darkening sun and sky. And out of the smoke fearsome locusts come to plague for five months all who do not bear the seal of God on their foreheads (9:1–6). This particular judgment is called the "first woe" (9:12); two additional woes will yet come.

6. Two hundred million mounted troops, but of strange description (see 9:17–19), kill a third of mankind (9:13–16).

A temple and two witnesses

Again there is an interlude. Chapter 10 describes an angel descending from heaven with a little scroll open in his hand. "Seven thunders" utter a message, but John is not permitted to record it (10:4). The angel promises that "in the days when the seventh angel is about to sound his trumpet, the mystery of God will be accomplished" (10:7).

The intermission continues. John is instructed to "measure the temple of God and the altar, and count the worshipers there" (11:1). Two "'witnesses'" are announced, who will "'prophesy for 1,260 days'" (11:3). They will be killed by "the beast that comes up from the Abyss" (11:7), but after three and a half days they will come to life and go up to heaven (11:11–12). A violent earthquake that will destroy a tenth of Jerusalem (we know John refers to Jerusalem, for he has just identified the city as the locus of Jesus' crucifixion—11:8) concludes the second woe (11:13–14).

7. The seventh trumpet judgment and the third woe announce the transfer of world sovereignty to "'our Lord and . . . his Christ [who] will reign for ever and ever'" (11:15). This would appear to be the consummation of all things, to which the church has looked forward for 1,900 years.

The woman and the dragon

There follows in chapter 12 a "sign" in heaven—a woman, who seems to be Israel, pursued by "an enormous red dragon" (12:3) who tries to devour the son she gives birth to (identified in 12:5 as "a male child, who will rule all the nations with an iron scepter"). The child escapes by being "snatched up to God and to his throne" (12:5); the woman finds nourishment for 1,260 days in the "desert" (12:6). And in heaven Michael and his angels succeed in overpowering the dragon and his angels, who are "hurled to the earth" (12:13). Frustrated in their attempts to harm the woman, they make war against "the rest of her offspring—those who obey God's commandments and hold to the testimony of Jesus" (12:17; cf. 1:9).

The two beasts

Next in John's vision come two beasts—one out of the sea (13:1) and one out of the earth (13:11). These beasts, who can be none other than Antichrist and his false prophet (cf. 20:10), make war against the "saints" (13:7) and obtain the worship of "all whose names have not been written in the book of life" (13:8). Only those bearing the mark of the beast on their right hand or forehead will be able to buy or sell (13:17)—economic pressure that will prove powerfully persuasive. The beast has a number. "His number is 666" (13:18).

The harvest of the earth

The Lamb, standing on Mount Zion, puts His seal on 144,000 of his specially identified people (14:1) who have "been redeemed from the earth" (14:3). Three angels appear, each with a specific proclamation to announce (see 14:6, 8, 9).

Then—awesome sight—John sees "one 'like a son of man,'" sharp sickle in hand, ready to reap the ripe "'harvest of the earth'" (14:15). "So he that was seated on the cloud swung his sickle over the earth, and the earth was harvested" (14:16).

Another angel, also with a sharp sickle, prepares to "'gather the clusters of grapes from the earth's vine'" (14:18). He swings his sickle on the earth, gathering the grapes, and throws them "into the great winepress of God's wrath" (14:19). The two-stage harvest has been reaped.

The seven "bowl" judgments

The scene shifts again to heaven, where John sees "those who had been victorious over the beast and his image and over the number of his name" (15:2). Then the "tabernacle of Testimony" opens (15:5) and seven angels come forth with "seven golden bowls filled with the wrath of God" (15:6–7).

1. "Ugly and painful sores" break out "on the people who had the mark of the beast and worshiped his image" (16:2).

2. The sea turns into "blood like that of a dead man," causing "every living thing in the sea" to die (16:3).

3. The "rivers and springs of water" become blood (16:4).

4. The sun is given "power to scorch people with fire" (16:8).

5. The kingdom of the beast is "plunged into darkness" (16:10).

6. The waters of the Euphrates River are "dried up to prepare the way for the kings from the East" (16:12).

7. A "loud voice from the throne" in the temple cries, "'It is done!'" (16:17). The most severe earthquake "since man has been on earth" splits "the great city" into three parts and collapses the "cities of the nations." All islands flee away and the mountains cannot be found. "Huge hailstones of about a hundred pounds each" fall on men (16:18–21).

The judgment of "Babylon"

Chapters 17 and 18 are devoted to a description of, and comment on, the destruction of "Babylon." Whether this is the literal city of Babylon, rebuilt sometime prior to this prophecy, or whether it is figurative language, we are not specifically told. It was a code word for Rome during the era of Roman persecutions, and the "seven hills" mentioned in 17:9 are a further hint that the angel talking to John is referring to

Rome, the city of seven hills.

From chapter 18 we understand that Babylon was an adulterous city (18:3), a luxurious city (18:9), a city of power (18:10), a commercial city (18:11–13), a wealthy city (18:14), a port city (18:17–19).

Actually it is not a city that John first sees, but a "woman sitting on a scarlet beast" (17:3). She is identified as "the great city that rules over the kings of the earth" (17:18)—at the time, Rome. She has a special name on her forehead (17:5), and John can see that she is "drunk with the blood of the saints, the blood of those who bore testimony to Jesus" (17:6). Her destruction is graphically described in chapter 18.

In heaven, "Hallelujahs"

The long-awaited victory over "'the great prostitute / who corrupted the earth by her adulteries'" (19:2) brings a mighty shout from a "great multitude in heaven" (19:1).

> *"Hallelujah!*
> *For our Lord God Almighty reigns.*
> *Let us rejoice and be glad,*
> *and give him glory!*
> *For the wedding of the Lamb has come,*
> *and his bride has made herself ready"*
>
> 19:6–7.

The triumphant note continues as one called "Faithful and True," astride "a white horse" (19:11) and bearing the name, "the Word of God" (19:13), charges forth with His army in white to "tread the winepress of the fury of the wrath of God Almighty" (19:15). In the resulting battle the beast and false prophet are captured and thrown "alive into the fiery lake of burning sulfur" (19:20).

With these out of the way, Satan is also seized, bound and locked into the Abyss for a thousand years (20:1–3), paving the way for Jesus' 1,000-year reign on earth with those who "have part in the first resurrection" (20:6).

The New Jerusalem

Satan has one more respite. "Released from his prison," he goes out "to deceive the nations in the four corners of the earth" and to "gather them for battle" (20:7–8). As numberless as "the sand on the seashore," they surround "the city [God] loves" (20:8–9). "Fire" from heaven devours them, and the devil who deceived them is "thrown into the lake of burning sulfur, where the beast and the false prophet" are, to be "tormented day and night for ever and ever" (20:9–10).

On a great white throne, God sits to judge "the dead, great and small" (20:11–12). "If anyone's name was not found written in the book of life, he was thrown into the lake of fire" (20:15).

"Then," John says, "I saw a new heaven and a new earth. . . . I saw the Holy City, the new Jerusalem, coming down out of heaven from God. . . . And I heard a loud voice from the throne saying, 'Now the dwelling of God is with men, and he will live with them. They will be his people, and God himself will be with them and be their God'" (21:1–3). And in that setting of peace and praise, God's servants "will reign for ever and ever" (22:5).

"'Behold, I am coming soon!'"

Three times Jesus says it: "'I am coming soon!'" (22:7, 12, 20).

This great book of prophecy ends with an invitation: "The Spirit and the bride say, 'Come!' And let him who hears say,

'Come!' Whoever is thirsty, let him come; and whoever wishes, let him take the free gift of the water of life" (22:17).

It ends also with a prayer: "Come, Lord Jesus" (22:20).

And with a benediction: "The grace of the Lord Jesus be with God's people. Amen" (22:21).

"Second mile" questions and topics

1. Not only is there a blessing promised to the reader of Revelation (1:3), but there is a warning to any who will either add to or take away from this book (22:18–19). Why do you suppose God inspired the writer to add that warning?

2. Roughly sketch out the throne room scene described in 4:2–11.

3. In 14:14–20 the "harvest" of earth is described. Compare this description with that in Jesus' parable of the weeds (Matthew 13:24–30, 37–42). What difference do you find in the sequence of events in the parable from the actual predicted event?